Endorsements

"This book is a strategic redirect—away from distraction and toward the only assets that survive death: truth, people, and your soul's alignment. If you're playing for legacy, not applause, this is your field guide."
— **Jeffrey Slayter, International Speaker and Author**

"Bruce captures the essence of biblical Christianity in a clear, concise, practical manner. Expressed through encouraging life stories of men and women of faith, along with clear diagrams of what walking by grace through faith looks like, Bruce presents the rich truth of a believer's life in Christ and Christ's life lived through the believer."
— **Erik Christensen, Pastor**

"I am excited for followers of Christ to enjoy this book and to apply the eternal applications and themes. I feel confident it will change people for the better as they consider their future."
— **Terry Looper, Author of Sacred Pace, Founder of Texon LP**

"Having known Bruce Witt for over 25 years, I can honestly say that Live for What Lasts is his best work yet. He delivers on paper, through the power of the Holy Spirit, a practical guidebook to living a life worth living. Way to go Bruce!!"
— **Trey Miller, President & CEO, Southern Andiron & Tool Co.**

ENDORSEMENTS

"Reading this book felt like having a trusted guide taking me by the hand and lifting my eyes beyond the distractions of today into the reality of eternity. It is not just theory, it is deeply practical, filled with stories, insights, and a framework that helps us reorient our lives around what truly matters.

"Bruce, a dear friend and fellow traveler with me in the Middle East, writes with both authority and humility. He has lived what he teaches, and his leadership reflects the very truths on these pages. This book will challenge you, encourage you, and most importantly, help you live a life of eternal impact. I wholeheartedly recommend it."

— Dr. Wahid Wahba. Founder and President 4G3

"I've known Bruce for decades, and what I've always admired most is that he doesn't just talk about eternal priorities—he lives them. This book is not theory or abstract teaching; it's a heartfelt invitation from someone who has wrestled with what truly matters and chosen to live for what lasts.

"I spent a lifetime as a financial advisor, and I saw firsthand how is easy to get caught up in the temporary—chasing things that fade. This book shows that real joy and freedom come when we align our lives with eternal values and God's purpose for our lives!

"If you want your life to count—not just for today, but forever—you need to read this book. It will push you closer to Christ, reframe how you view success, and remind you of the incredible joy that awaits when we hear those words, 'Well done, good and faithful servant.' I'm grateful for this powerful message, and how God continues to use Bruce in a mighty way!"

— David Ward, Wealth Advisor

Live For What Lasts

"Live for What Lasts *is a timely and powerful book that calls us to lift our eyes above the temporary and fix them on the eternal. Bruce Witt, a friend, mentor, and life coach, writes with both deep biblical conviction and practical clarity. His message is not theory—it is truth lived out and tested.*

"In these pages, Bruce helps us understand what it truly means to surrender our lives, to appropriate the riches we already have in Christ, and to be led daily by the Spirit. The result is not striving harder in our own strength, but living with the freedom, joy, and purpose that flow from God's grace.

"This book is more than a resource—it's a roadmap for anyone who longs to live with an eternal perspective and for eternal rewards. I wholeheartedly recommend it to every believer who desires to go deeper with Christ and to make their life count for what will truly last."

— **Thinus Botha, Chief Ministry Officer, Harvesters Ministries**

LIVE FOR WHAT LASTS

SHIFT YOUR PERSPECTIVE...OUR BEST IS YET TO COME

BRUCE R. WITT

THE COACHING LEADER

Live For What Lasts
Shift Your Perspective...Our Best Is Yet to Come

Copyright © 2025 by Bruce R. Witt

All Rights Reserved. No portion of this book may be reproduced, stored in a retrieval system, or transmitted in any form or by any means—electronic, mechanical, photocopy, recording, scanning, or other—except for brief quotations in critical reviews or articles, without the prior written permission of the publisher.

ISBN: 978-1-7340079-2-3

Unless otherwise noted, Scripture quotations are from the NEW AMERICAN STANDARD BIBLE®, Copyright © 1960, 1962, 1963, 1968, 1971, 1972, 1973, 1975, 1977, 1995 by The Lockman Foundation. Used by permission.

Scripture quotations marked (KJV) are from the King James Version.

Scripture quotations marked (MSG) are from The Message. Copyright © 1993, 1994, 1995, 1996, 2000, 2001, 2002. Used by permission of NavPress Publishing Group.

Scripture quotations marked (NIV) are from THE HOLY BIBLE, NEW INTERNATIONAL VERSION®, NIV® Copyright © 1973, 1978, 1984, 2011 by Biblica, Inc.® Used by permission. All rights reserved worldwide.

Scripture quotations marked (NLT) are from the Holy Bible, New Living Translation, copy¬right © 1996, 2004, 2015 by Tyndale House Foundation. Used by permission of Tyndale House Publishers, Inc., Carol Stream, Illinois 60188. All rights reserved.

Published by Leadership Revolution Inc.

Learn more at www.LeadershipRevolution.us

Interior Layout: Kaci Ariza

Cover Design: Michael Sean Allen

Leadership Revolution, Inc.
Bruce Witt, President
4465 Nassau Way
Marietta, GA 30068
678-637-9890

Bruce@LeadershipRevolution.us
www.LeadershipRevolution.us

November 2025 Printing

Contents

Introduction		3
Chapter 1	The Echo of Eternity	5
Chapter 2	We are Made for Eternity	9
Chapter 3	Change: Imitation vs. Transformation	15
Chapter 4	Shift #1 Christ Like to Christ Life	25
Chapter 5	Shift #2 For Christ to From Christ	39
Chapter 6	Shift #3 Achieve to Receive	53
Chapter 7	Shift #4 King to Kingdom	67
Chapter 8	Shift #5 Trials to Triumph	81
Chapter 9	Eternal Impact	93
Chapter 10	Practical Impact Framework	99
Chapter 11	Finishing Well to Entering into the Joy of the Master	105
Chapter 12	A Call to Action	113
About the Author		121

Live For What Lasts

Live For What Lasts
Shift Your Perspective ... Our Best Is Yet to Come

Introduction

"We look upon the time we have as our own, and feel free to use it for what we like. But the Bible makes it plain that our time belongs to God and should be spent on the things that last forever."
— Oswald Chambers

"For here we do not have an enduring city, but we are looking for the city that is to come." **— Hebrews 13:14**

We live in a world obsessed with the temporary—chasing achievements, accumulating possessions, and curating moments that vanish as quickly as they come. But deep down, we all sense it: not everything we pour our lives into will live on. The question that changes everything is this:

What truly lasts forever?

The Bible answers with clarity and hope. There are five things that will carry into eternity:

1. An intimate relationship with Christ.
2. God's unchanging Word.
3. The spirit and soul of people.
4. The rewards we will be given in heaven.
5. Our worship, praise, and thanksgiving to God Himself.

> *How we live our lives on earth will directly affect the quality of our life in eternity.*

What difference will this make in your life?

When these five things become the central priorities of our hearts, minds, and daily actions, something extraordinary happens—we begin to live for what counts most. Our lives take on eternal significance and impact. We glorify the Lord in ways that will bless us forever. We will stand before Him to those longed-for words: *"Well done, good and faithful servant. You have been faithful in a few things; I will give you much."* And greater than those words, we will be invited into experiencing a deepening intimacy with Christ forever: *"Enter into the joy of your master."*

This book is an invitation—a challenge—to reorder your life around what will matter forever. It's not simply about believing in life beyond the temporal; it's about living in light of eternity. The best part is that it will radically enhance your life here and there. Each chapter will help you make practical, faith-filled changes so that your time, energy, and resources are invested in what will never fade. Remember not everything that you accumulate or accomplish in this life will live on, it will be tested and evaluated which will reveal if it has the stamp of eternity.

You only get one life. Make it count for what lasts.

At the heart of the roadmap for this book are five shifts that will not only change how you live, but who you become. They are not spiritual enhancements. They are invitations into the life you were always meant to live:

1. Move From "Christlike" to "Christ Life" → Shift in the Power and the Source → WHO?
2. Redirect your focus of "For Christ" to "From Christ" → Shift your Purpose and Relationships → WHY?
3. Exchange Achieving to Receiving → Shift our Actions and Work → WHAT?
4. Casting down the King to Serving the Kingdom → Shift your Focus and Audience → HOW?
5. Reframe your focus From Trials to Triumph. → Shift from Problems to God's Victorious Work → WHICH?

Chapter One

The Echo of Eternity

"What we do in life, echoes in eternity." — **Maximus, in Gladiator**

"Do not store up for yourselves treasures on earth...But store up for yourselves treasures in heaven. Where your treasure is your heart will be also" — **Matthew 6:19–21**

Our vision of the new life is not just a belief tucked away in the back of our minds—it is the compass that absolutely governs every choice, every desire, and every pursuit in this life. What we truly believe about forever will inevitably shape how we live right now.

The sobering reality is that much of what fills our days—though enjoyable, respectable, even useful—may have no weight in heaven. Success here does not always translate into significance there. And that should stop every follower of Christ long enough to ask: *Why am I doing what I am doing? What will last when this life is over?*

Jesus spoke with piercing clarity: *"Do not store up for yourselves treasures on earth... But store up for yourselves treasures in heaven."* His words are not mere suggestion; they are a reorientation of our hearts toward the true economy of God—a call to live in such a way that our actions impact infinity.

The Big Idea of This Book

Your life and legacy can carry lasting significance if you will allow God to transform your perspective and your actions. You were made for more than comfort, more than the race for recognition, more than the quiet resignation of simply surviving. In Christ, both your *now* and your *forever* can glorify the Lord, fulfill His purposes, and bless you forever.

This is not about adding more to your schedule. It is about replacing the temporary with the eternal, the trivial with the truly important. It is about trading the fading applause of earth for the enduring reward of heaven. It will take a change of beliefs and perspectives to make changes in your actions.

The Need of the Hour

The hour in which we live is urgent. Followers of Christ must reclaim the priority of what truly counts. Yet we are bombarded—distracted by endless streams of information, tangled in the increasing velocity of technology, and dulled by the pursuit of pleasure that subtly become chains. Meanwhile, the forces of darkness are not sleeping. Evil is escalating. The cry of the last, the least, and the lost is rising all around us.

And yet—there is hope and Christ is that hope. Every person in the world needs Christ, and He is the peace the restless soul is searching for. He is the only One who can take what is temporary and turn it into something eternal.

The call of this book is simple but costly: ***Live for What Lasts.*** Lift your eyes beyond the horizon of this world and anchor your heart to the Kingdom that cannot be shaken. For the best is yet to come—but only for those who refuse to spend their lives on what will not follow them home. You will be challenged to make some deep changes.

We all will give an account at the end of our earthly lives of what we did with what we have been given. The Lord will judge our faithfulness to the opportunities given us. The standard will not be a comparison or who produced the most, it will be did we do our very best.

Thinus Botha - A Life Poured Out for What Lasts

My friend Thinus Botha from Boksburg, South Africa, lives out an eternal pursuit as he serves the Lord planting churches across East Africa. He fearlessly shares Christ in war-torn nations like Mozambique and the Congo, in Muslim-influenced regions of Uganda and Zanzibar, and in more peaceful countries such as Ethiopia and Kenya.

Humble Beginnings

Born in Johannesburg's working-class Newlands neighborhood, Thinus grew up in poverty and brokenness. His father was unfaithful, then died of cancer when Thinus was just 14. His mother raised four children alone, stretching every cent to survive. From age 11, Thinus worked to help support the family. Ashamed of his circumstances, he found refuge at night when his mother read from a small blue children's Bible — planting seeds of faith in his heart.

Loss and Loneliness

After his father's death, his mother's new relationship created distance with her children, leaving young Thinus to largely fend for himself. He threw himself into sports to escape the ache of loneliness, but resentment grew. In high school, a teacher introduced him to Jesus personally, and he prayed to receive Christ. Yet with no discipleship, he drifted into the wrong crowd. By his late teens, heartbroken and hopeless, he even planned to end his life. But in that darkest night, God intervened. Thinus later recognized it as grace.

A New Surrender

By 21, he knew he could not live for himself any longer. He recommitted his life to Christ and was discipled by a local pastor. It was then he sensed a call to the nations — a call he could not ignore. At 27, after selling everything he owned, he set out for Mozambique with only a backpack and Bible. For two years he lived under a tree in rural villages, facing malaria, snakes, witch doctors, and hunger. At first, he thought God had sent him there to die. But when he began gathering people under that tree, thirty-seven came, and a church was born. Soon, more villages asked for churches, and the gospel began to spread.

Redirected but Not Forgotten

God later led Thinus back to Johannesburg for formal study. Funding himself by making and selling biltong, he enrolled at seminary. Though unexpectedly appointed to staff at a large church, he continued to carry the burden for unreached nations. For over a decade he served as Outreach and then Executive Pastor, until God opened the door to join Harvesters Ministries, a global movement focused on church planting and training pastors.

Why He Lives for the Eternal

When asked why he pours out his life this way, Thinus points to Abraham, who lived in tents while looking for the eternal city of God. He describes this life as temporary, like a tent, while the reward is eternal. "It's better to cry now and laugh later," he often says. "Some laugh now, but they'll cry later. If you keep your eyes on the winning post — on Christ — you can endure anything."

For Thinus, the cost is nothing compared to the joy of seeing churches planted, disciples multiplied, and Christ exalted among the nations. His life is proof that when surrendered fully, God can use even humble beginnings to shape eternal impact.

This story is an invitation — to trust that nothing surrendered to God is ever wasted, and to live now for what will is eternal.

Chapter Two

We are Made for Eternity

"He is no fool who gives what he cannot keep to gain that which he cannot lose." — **Jim Elliot**

"For whoever wishes to save his life will lose it; but whoever loses his life for My sake will find it. For what will it profit a man if he gains the whole world and forfeits his soul? Or what will a man give in exchange for his soul?" — **Matthew 16:25–26**

Jim Elliot wrote this in his journal in 1949, years before giving his life as a missionary to the Huaorani people in Ecuador. It is a beautiful picture of letting go temporary things for eternal gain.

A Life Too Small

The great tragedy of our day is not that the world is broken—that much we expect. The greater tragedy is that many Christians live as if this broken world is their only reality. They believe in heaven but live like earth is all there is. They carry the Spirit of God within them yet operate by the mindset and patterns of a self-reliant world. They've inherited the abundance of Christ but live like spiritual paupers.

We've confused activity with intimacy. We've mistaken imitation for the indwelling of the Holy Spirit. And in our zeal to serve God, we've often disconnected from the Source of life itself. The result? Sincere but weary believers—full of motion but short on significance. Emotionally depleted, spiritually dry, and far from the joy, power, and freedom the New Testament describes. We've settled for a manageable version of Christianity that conforms to the world's rhythms instead of being transformed by the Spirit's renewing work.

Paul's words in Romans 12:1–2 leave no room for such small living: *"Therefore I urge you, brethren, by the mercies of God, to present your bodies a living and holy sacrifice… Do not be conformed to this world, but be transformed by the renewing of your mind…"*

This is not a call to tweak your schedule or clean up a few habits. Paul is calling for a complete reorientation—from conformity to transformation, from behavior modification to spiritual metamorphosis. The problem for many Christians today is not a lack of salvation but a lack of dying to self. We've embraced forgiveness but stopped short of freedom

It's time to return to the heart of the gospel—not merely that Christ died for you, but that He lives in you. The best is not just what God will do for you, but what He longs to do through you.

My Story: From Driven to Dependent

I know this journey well—because I've lived it. Raised with a strong work ethic, I believed success was earned. And in many ways, it worked.

I grew up in Fairfield, Montana, a small, rural farming community in the foothills of the Rocky Mountains. Growing up, our family did not attend church, Sunday was a day to play. It was ideal in many ways, yet I longed for more. I attended Montana State University in Bozeman, Montana, a small college town nestled in the mountains and now is a place where many seek to live. All we could think about was getting out of there.

During college I started a business selling books door-to-door and was quite successful. I graduated near the top of my class in engineering, succeeded in athletics, and was rewarded, respected, and admired. From there I made my break, I went to work for a division of Shell Oil Company and moved to Houston, Texas, and started up the corporate ladder and was influenced by many top-level businesspeople along the way. As a young man, I held numerous leadership positions in both college organizations and in community endeavors. Being a self-starter, I took on as many responsibilities as I could at Shell.

By now, I was in my early twenties and had everything a person would want great income, position, possession, and many friends. Yet I was empty on the inside, so I began to search for answers. Having met several businesspeople who were Christians, I began to ask many questions. They shared with me about Jesus Christ and the bible. I came to an understanding that I was separated from Christ because of sin and falling short. They taught me about prayer and so I prayed asking Christ to save me of my sin, forgive and receive eternal life.

When I became a Christian, I simply transferred that drive into my faith. I served fervently. I worked hard to "make a difference for God." An older couple soon began to disciple my wife and me which resulted in significant spiritual growth. We were fully engaged in the ministry of evangelism and discipleship. My career and my life were doing quite well and from a world perspective I was very successful. My view was that the Lord and I made a good team – I worked hard so that He would bless me.

When the Lord called me into vocational Christian work with a marketplace ministry, I thought I truly had something to offer given my past success in the marketplace. In addition, I was very committed to expanding God's Kingdom. I had a feeling that joining up with the Lord was going to be a great thing. My wife and I moved from Atlanta, GA to Houston, TX with two young boys, when we started into ministry. We did not know the rough waters that faced us, more on this later.

Within days of the move, life began to turn upside down and in only a couple of months the wheels came off the wagon. I was exhausted, frustrated, and struggling to make my spiritual life and my leadership work. I felt like a failure and was ashamed of my thoughts and feelings. I was at the end of my rope and had nowhere else to turn. So, I turned to the Lord who had always been with me. I cried out, "I am fit to quit." I sincerely loved Jesus—but I was exhausted. I believed I was honoring God by giving Him everything I had. But eventually, I had nothing left.

That's when I encountered the teachings of men like Major Ian Thomas and Wayne Barber—men who lived the truth I had never fully grasped: The Christian life is not me trying to live for Christ. It is Christ living His life through me. It was then that I made the GREAT DISCOVERY: <u>God did not need me,</u> yet He did want to use me. God wanted to work in and through me to accomplish His work. I was valued and loved for who I was in Christ. My security, significance, and acceptance were not based on my performance, but on what Christ did. What a revelation!

My struggle was not a punishment for wrongdoing or for being a sinner. In fact, it demonstrated God's grace in that He wanted me to grow in my relationship with Him so that He could manifest His power through my weakness. This was both humbling and freeing. I was a saint in God's eyes, although I sinned and was in need of help.

The Christian life was much more about having an intimate relationship with Him and to know His life in me than it was just trying harder to be like Jesus. I did not have to perform or strive in order to gain God's blessing and presence. I began to understand that He was not only my forgiveness, but He was also my source of everything I needed to function in life.

What a sense of relief and freedom that I began to take hold of. I was released from the bondage of legalistic Christians who were trying hard to jump through hoops and conform to their convictions. My busyness turned into rest, and my struggle turned into fruitfulness.

The difference has been everything. Slowly, I began to exchange drivenness for dependence, performance for presence, self-effort for abiding. My external success no longer defined me. My intimacy with Christ did. Ministry stopped being an obligation and became overflow. And I discovered that the life I had always longed for wasn't achieved by striving—it was attained through dying.

I began to discover that I was made for more – a life that impacts eternity now, and forever.

How We Were Designed

God designed you for more than the few decades you spend on this earth. You are an eternal being—created in His image, redeemed by His Son, indwelt by His Spirit—and destined to live forever. This means your choices, priorities, and pursuits were never meant to be measured only by time; they were always meant to be measured by what never stops forever.

When we live with the next life in view, our lives gain a deeper clarity and purpose. The fog of distraction begins to lift, and the petty urgencies that once consumed us lose their grip.

Living an infinite life inspires us to desire deeper intimacy with the Lord. We begin to see Him not as a distant deity to be served out of duty, but as the Treasure of our souls. Our relationship with Him becomes the wellspring of every decision and the joy behind every act of obedience.

It focuses our hearts on living with God's purposes in mind. The question shifts from "What do I want out of life?" to "What and how does God want to use me?" That shift reframes every goal, every dollar, and every moment in light of His Kingdom.

It teaches us to prioritize the good, better, and best. When the next life is the measure, we are less impressed with what is merely good, more eager to pursue what is better, and ultimately committed to what is best—the will of God.

It redeems and leverages our pain for good. Every wound, loss, and trial become a seed that, in God's hands, produces growth. Our brokenness is not wasted—it becomes part of someone else's healing, a testimony to His redeeming power.

It builds our faith in the face of opposition. When trials come, we can endure—not because the pain is easy, but because we know it is temporary. The storms of life can deepen our roots instead of washing us away.

An Eternal Impact

We are eternal beings living in a temporary world. The danger is that we confuse the two—and end up living for what will not last. But when we live with a clear focus on life after death, our impact becomes multi-purposed and far-reaching.

Eternal impact is more than a concept—it is the reality that the way you live today will change forever in God's purposes. Every prayer whispered in faith, every sacrifice made in love, every word spoken in truth, every burden carried with grace—none of it is wasted. Heaven will reveal the full story.

And on that day, when you see Christ face to face, you will know that living for what lasts was worth it all.

A Final Word: Your Invitation

This book is not about adding more to your life—it's about giving away your life entirely. Not so you can do less, but so Christ has great things in store for you. You don't need to fix your life; you need to give up control of your life. This isn't self-help wrapped in Christian language. This is Christ at the center—His life, His power, His presence, His will.

You were made for more than busyness, burnout, and survival. You were made to walk in intimacy, purpose, and power. You were made to experience the indwelling life of Christ—and to impact eternity as He lives through you. So, I invite you now—not to try harder, but to give up completely.

It's *within you*. It's Christ in you.

In the pages ahead, I'll share the five foundational shifts that changed everything for me. They reshaped my perspective, restored my joy, and reoriented my life around what truly lasts. They will do the same for you—if you are willing to exchange a life too small for a life that echoes with infinite power.

Chapter Three
Change: Imitation vs. Transformation

"Let us give up our work, our plans, ourselves, our lives, our loved ones, our influence…all, right into God's hand — and then when we have given all over to Him, there will be nothing left for us to be troubled about." — **Hudson Taylor**

"Therefore, I urge you, brethren, by the mercies of God, to present your bodies a living and holy sacrifice, acceptable to God, which is your spiritual service of worship. And do not be conformed to this world, but be transformed by the renewing of your mind, so that you may prove what the will of God is, that which is good and acceptable and perfect." — **Romans 12:1-2**

Many believers live their spiritual lives from the outside in. They look to circumstances, performance, reputation, or feelings to define their spiritual state. When life goes well, they feel close to God. When they fail, they feel farther apart. They approach spiritual growth like a project: read more, try harder, serve better. And still, they feel stuck. Why is this?

Imitation – Outside – In Change

Outward change is most often trying be be like someone – imitation. It is what the world suggests and pursues, it is captured in this quote, *"Sow a thought and you reap an action; sow an act and you reap a habit; sow a habit and you reap a character; sow a character and you reap a destiny." Ralph Waldo Emerson.* As good as it sounds and works in the short term, but it does not bring lasting change.

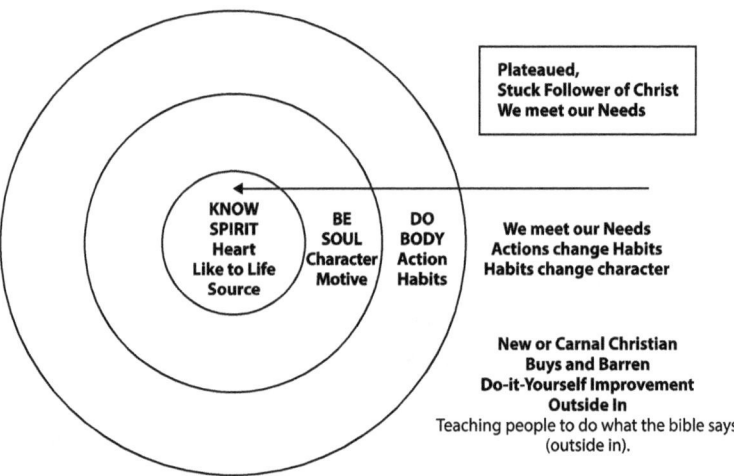

When we look at our circumstances first, our feelings and perspective fuel our behavior. This outward looking view magnifies these emotions and our thinking driving us to meet our needs and try harder to overcome in our strength. This outside-in process begins with what we bring to the table: our self-effort, our strength, our desires, and talents. If we function in these primarily, it will lead to a busy life with to show for it and we become plateaued, stuck in our way of thinking. In general, we're trying to live life in the best way we can. It is the ultimate do-it-yourself improvement process which only leads to frustration and emptiness.

This perspective is common for both the new and carnal Christian because it relies on the flesh and is a product of the world. The consequences include: being led by their needs, walking by sight, focus on measuring and comparing, influenced by circumstances, and decision making is more feeling than faith.

Transformation – Inside – Out Change

The gospel invites us to live from the inside out. To allow the indwelling Christ to shape our thinking, align our emotions, purify our desires, and empower our actions. It is not you becoming more Christlike by your own effort—it is Christ expressing His life through you by His power. Galatians 2:20 guides us—it's a spiritual blueprint: *"I have been crucified with Christ; and it is no longer I who live, but Christ lives in me..."*

This is the great exchange. Your old life, with all its striving, insecurity, and sin, has been put to death. In its place, Christ lives His life through you—not as a moral ideal, but as a living reality. This renewal is not self-improvement; it is self-surrender. And the moment you begin to live from Christ rather than merely for Christ, everything changes.

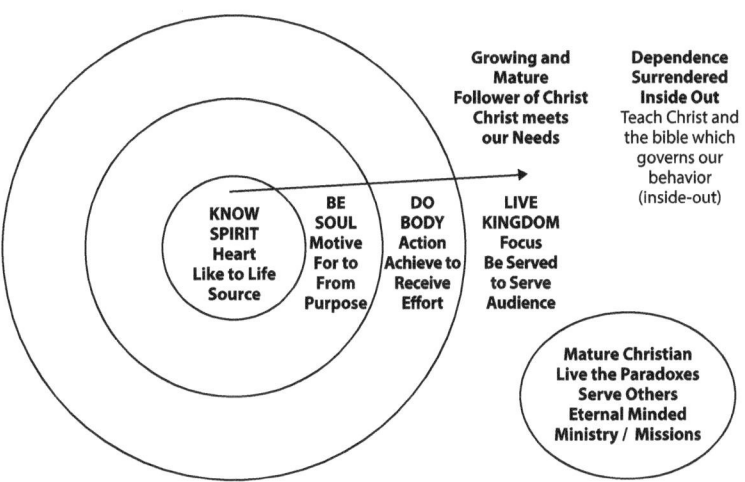

This new way is characterized by a deep dependence and faith in Christ and not who we are in our human bodies. Christ and all of His provisions are released through emptiness and brokenness. When we come to the end of our limited resources and strength it allows Christ to work through us and meet our needs. This is called maturity, it is where we serve others, we have an eternal mindset, and our life is filled with a sense of ministry and mission as we work in God's Kingdom.

The reshaped life begins on the inside it moves to the successive layers outward. It begins in the spirit where we know Christ by experience or know Him intimately (Phil 3:8-10). It is our heart, and it is the source of all that we gain from Christ (life, power, wisdom, vision). This is who we are because the Holy Spirit is our innermost being and God looks at us as being righteous.

From this sense of being and new character, we move to doing which is a sense of fulfilling God's will and not achievement in our strengths, our talents, and our experiences. This focus on doing God's will gives us a purpose and cause to live life in the world and be a light in the midst of darkness. We need to see this world as God's Kingdom, and we are called to be servants in it.

Five Foundational Shifts that will Change your Spiritual Life.

This book outlines five changes of perspective:

1. ***Move From "Christlike" to "Christ Life" (Shift in the Power and the Source)***

   For many Christians, the highest aspiration is to be more like Jesus. We wear the bracelets. We ask, "What would Jesus do?" We aim to imitate His life. But here's the problem: ***you can't imitate the Son of God in your own strength.*** Trying to be like Jesus without the life of Jesus is crushing. The source of the Christian life is not *you becoming more like Christ*. It is *Christ becoming your life*.

   The Lord works through the humble to accomplish His purposes and establish His Church. We are called to die which is reflected through our **CORE VALUES** such as humility, other-centeredness, and sacrifice. The power comes as you appropriate Christ as your source of life. This first shift will exponentially grow our impact because the source moves from finite to infinite. Yet this is only found when we die to the flesh often and keep trusting.

2. **Redirect your focus of "For Christ" to "From Christ" (Shift your Purpose and Relationships)**

    Many Christians wake up each day trying to do something *for* God. To prove their worth. To demonstrate their devotion. To carry the weight of ministry or family or morality on their shoulders. But this is backwards. We weren't created to live for Christ. We were created to live from Christ. That's why Jesus said, *"Abide in Me… for apart from Me, you can do nothing" (John 15:5).* He didn't say, "You can't do much." He said, "You can do nothing."

    It is only in our intimate relationship with Christ that we find the foundation and fuel to grow. Christ produces the fruit flowing from the vine to the branches). The depth of our relationship with Christ will determine our breadth. Intimacy precedes ministry, an abiding relationship with Christ should be our **PURPOSE**. Christ is our life and our **"WHY"**.

3. **Exchange Achieving to Receiving (Shift our Actions and Work)**

    Here's a hard truth: *you can't produce holiness from human effort.* No amount of Bible reading, church attendance, or spiritual discipline will ever be enough to make you holy in God's eyes. That's not to say those things aren't valuable—they are. But they were never meant to be the *source* of life. They are the *response* to it. We are not to "Achieve" things in our strength, we are to "Receive" His gifts and give them away.

    The Christian life and ministry begin with receiving not achieving, they both grow by giving and not holding on to them. Our receiving should be filled with thankfulness and humility. We will reap what we sow. Our **MISSION** is found in doing things with excellence and giving generously, both define our **"WHAT"**. Be a wise steward in exercising faith and planning.

4. ***Casting down the King to Serving the Kingdom (Shift your Focus and Audience)***
   The fourth shift moves us from being at the center to letting Christ and His kingdom guide and direct our hearts and action. Our impact is inversely proportional to our trying to control. High control leads to little influence, let the Lord control and know His on the throne and working yield high impact. Our role is faithful stewardship and be willing to be held accountable.

   The Lord purposes are to glorify Himself, establish His Kingdom, and to make disciples of all nations. We fit into His purposes and are not doing things to make us great. We are called to serve, not to be served. We are not to be in control and build great organizations. We are to set down to lift up. Our **VISION** is to serve and value people and reveals **"WHERE"** are going.

5. ***Reframe your focus From Trials to Triumph.***
   (Shift from Problems to God's Victorious Work)
   Don't let your problems, your flesh, or the opposition of the enemy thwart your growth. Stand firm and allow Christ to fight the battle in and through you. He will bring you to His peace. There is a blessing in brokenness and a ministry through pain. We must embrace the reality that life has difficulties.

   Embrace the journey, life will be difficult as we live in a fallen world, yet there is victory in the valley. The Lord allows and uses brokenness to being us to our end so that He can shape and grow us for His use. We must accept the suffering and learn from it. As we do, our ministry will flourish. Brokenness builds bridges, promoting our success builds walls. Our thankfulness in challenges helps us **EXECUTE a PLAN** with an unusual empathy to a world in need which becomes **"HOW"** we do life. Do not go alone.

Summary of the Five Foundational Changes

Exchange	Question	Spiritual Application	Results	Practical Action
Christ Like to Christ Life	WHO	Surrender / Appropriate	Power	Core Values
For to From	WHY	Abide / Depend	Fruit	Purpose
Achieve to Receive	WHAT	Thank / Give	Grace	Mission
King to Kingdom	HOW	Humble / Serve	Light	Vision
Trial to Triumph	WHICH	Rejoice / Press On	Growth	Execute your Plan

These shifts are not steps on a ladder, but lenses through which to see your life in Christ. They are not formulas. They are foundational truths. Each one leads you further from conformity to culture and deeper into communion with Christ. Let's see how this works.

Wayne Barber's Journey: A Life Well Lived. Moving From Performance to Presence

Wayne Barber was a dear and personal friend of mine. He also was admired as a pastor and teacher. He was beloved for his clarity, his heart, and his ability to unpack Scripture verse by verse in a way that nourished the soul. Yet what made his teaching so powerful wasn't just his communication skill—it was the depth of his death to the flesh. Like many leaders, Barber had seasons in ministry where the weight of doing for God became heavier than the joy of being with God. He had to learn the hard way that performance—even good performance for God—could not sustain the soul.

He once shared that the turning point came when he truly grasped that the Christian life was not about *imitating* Jesus, but about *participating* in His life. He came to a place of brokenness where his sufficiency ran dry—and Christ's sufficiency took over. From that point forward, his teaching took on a distinct shape: less about external discipline, and more about internal dependence.

Barber often said: *"The Christian life is not me trying to live for Christ, it's Christ living His life in and through me. The difference is everything."* This revelation realigned his ministry, his preaching, and his personal life. He began to speak with urgency and tenderness about the danger of religious activity apart from relational connectedness He warned of the trap of conformation—the pressure to look like a Christian on the outside while remaining unchanged on the inside.

Imitation vs. Transformation: What's the Difference?

Wayne Barber clearly distinguished between two types of spiritual lives: those shaped by conformation and those formed by transformation.

- **Imitation** is outward. It's about appearances, effort, imitation, and often rooted in fear or shame. You do the right things, say the right words, and maintain the image—but underneath, you're empty. You're being squeezed into a mold—by culture, religion, or your own expectations.
- **Transformation,** on the other hand, is inward. It is the Spirit of Christ renewing your mind, softening your heart, and reshaping your desires. It's not about acting differently—it's about *being made new.* This is not behavior modification. It is *soul reformation.*

Barber would often quote 2 Corinthians 3:18 to explain this process: *"We all, with unveiled face, beholding as in a mirror the glory of the Lord, are being transformed into the same image…"*

This is the inside-out life. It begins not with effort, but with *beholding.* Not with pressure, but with presence. It happens not because we try—but because we *trust.* Wayne Barber didn't finish well because he was strong. He finished well because he was had completely given up. He lived with an open Bible, an open heart, and a dependent spirit. *"God didn't call you to live for Him. He called you to let Him live in and through you. Don't let religion shape you from the outside in. Let Christ transform you from the inside out."*

He taught believers how to be at home with Christ, how to let the Word of God renew their minds, and how to respond to the Spirit rather than react to the world. This kind of life results in:

Clarity — because you're no longer driven by the demands of the world or religion.

Peace — because your worth and who you are, these have their roots in Christ's presence, not your performance.

Fruitfulness — not the forced kind, but the supernatural kind that flows from abiding (John 15:5).

Freedom — because you're no longer trying to be someone you're not—you're resting in who Christ is in you.

Barber often said that the Christian life isn't about *trying*, it's about trusting. It's about yielding control. It's about coming to the end of yourself so that Christ can begin to live His life through you.

CHANGE: OUTSIDE-IN OR INSIDE-OUT

Chapter Four

Shift #1
Christ Like to Christ Life
WHO?

"If Christ be anything, He must be everything. O rest not till love and faith in Jesus be the master passions of your soul!"
— **Charles Spurgeon**

"For you have died and your life is hidden with Christ in God. When Christ, who is our life, is revealed, then you also will be revealed with Him in glory…Christ is all and in all." — **Colossians 3:3-4,11**

Christ as Our Life: Living with His Indwelling Presence as the Source

The Christian life is not about trying to be like Jesus; it is about Christ Himself living His life within us. This is the foundational truth that separates religion from true spiritual renewal Many believers live under the exhausting burden of striving to imitate Christ—reading His words, emulating His actions, and attempting to conform their behavior to His example. Yet, the Scriptures reveal a far greater reality: ***Christ is not merely our model, He is our very life***, Colossians 3:4, "When Christ, who is our life, is revealed, then you also will be revealed with Him in glory."

"The Christian life is nothing less than the life which He lived then, lived now by Him in you! You cannot—He never said you could—but He can, and He always said He would!" Major Ian Thomas,

"Christianity is not about self-improvement but self-abandonment—recognizing that our old nature is incapable of producing the righteousness God requires, and only Christ in us can live the life we are called to." Ken Boa

The following life story of my friend, Jeff Slayter is a picture of this.

From Searching Everywhere to Finding the One Who Satisfies

Jeff was born in Honolulu, Hawaii, into a family that knew both love and struggle. Some of his earliest memories were of his grandmother bringing mangoes so they could eat, or of groceries being returned at the checkout line because the card didn't go through. His father worked hard, but the family's move from laid-back Hawaii to the driven culture of Silicon Valley only deepened the pressures.

A Faith That Didn't Fit

His family wasn't religious, so when Jeff was enrolled in a private Christian school, the version of God he encountered felt harsh and legalistic. Fear, not love, was at the center, and by age nine Jeff had turned away from Christianity entirely.

Searching Everywhere Else

As Jeff grew, his hunger for meaning pushed him far beyond conventional paths. He earned a business degree and built a strong real estate portfolio, only to lose it all in the 2008 crash. Money proved empty, so he searched for truth in self-improvement, meditation, and Eastern spirituality. He explored yoga, Hindu texts, mystical readings of Scripture, and later, psychedelics and shamanic practices across the world.

Alongside his explorations, his career soared. Jeff became a sought-after speaker on sales and human potential, sharing stages with Richard

Branson, Tony Robbins, and others. From the outside, he seemed successful. Inside, he was restless. No achievement, practice, or ceremony could fill the hole in his heart.

A Different Kind of Witness

The turning point didn't come through a sermon but through quiet Christian friends in Australia. They weren't judgmental or fearful; they lived with integrity and kindness. One invited Jeff to work out and began answering his questions patiently, never shutting him down. For the first time, Jeff encountered a faith that could handle his doubts.

Meeting Jesus

One night in his meditation room, Jeff prayed: "Jesus, if You are real, I only want You here. No other spirits, no other guides. Just You." Nothing dramatic happened in the moment, but soon evidence of God's presence became undeniable. His wife also began rediscovering Scripture, and together they felt the pull of the Holy Spirit.

Through study and prayer, Jeff realized that if Christianity was true, everything else was secondary. Together with his wife, he surrendered to Christ. Weeks later, they were baptized side by side in a friend's pool in Australia.

A New Foundation

Following Jesus meant dismantling the identity Jeff had built as a guru and thought leader. Yet what could have felt like loss became freedom. Returning to America, he and his wife began humbly, living simply, leading small Bible studies, and discipling others coming out of New Age practices.

Today, God has brought Jeff back to the stage, but with a new foundation. His teaching no longer points to self-help but to biblical truth and God's wisdom. Some who listen come to Christ, others don't—but Jeff's role is simply to be a faithful witness.

Living for What Lasts

Looking back, Jeff sees his long search—through money, success, mysticism, and psychedelics—as a journey that led him to the only One who satisfies. "How could I know myself if I didn't know my Creator? We become what we worship. And I'm so grateful now to worship a God who loves me so much."

Jeff Slayter's story is a reminder to seekers everywhere: you can chase every path the world offers, but until you surrender to Christ, the hole in your heart will remain. In Him, Jeff finally found the truth, freedom, and love he had searched for all his life. The Christian life is not one of outward performance but one of an intimate relationship.

Christ: The Source of Our Life

Throughout Scripture, we see that Christ is not just the giver of life but **the very essence of life itself**. He is the source of:

Life – The new, eternal, and abundant life we have in Him.

Power – The supernatural ability to live a victorious Christian life.

Vision – Spiritual sight to discern His will and purpose.

Wisdom – Divine understanding to navigate life in accordance with His truth.

Leadership – The ability to influence others through His Spirit rather than fleshly charisma.

Righteousness – A right standing before God, given as a gift, not earned by effort.

Provision – All that is necessary for life and godliness.

Strength – The ability to endure trials and serve in His power rather than our own.

Biblical Foundations of Christ as Our Life

This theme is deeply embedded in Scripture. Christ's sufficiency and our full dependence on Him are revealed in six ways.

1. **Christ's Life in Us: The Source of Our Strength**
   Paul teaches in Ephesians that we are strengthened through the Spirit—not through our own efforts. The goal is not self-improvement but Spirit-empowered change, leading to Christ dwelling in us by faith. The ultimate purpose is to be filled with all the fullness of God, which is not a state we achieve but a reality we receive by surrender.

   "That He would grant you, according to the riches of His glory, to be strengthened with power through His Spirit in the inner man, so that Christ may dwell in your hearts through faith; and that you, being rooted and grounded in love, may be able to comprehend with all the saints what is the breadth and length and height and depth, and to know the love of Christ which surpasses knowledge, that you may be filled up to all the fullness of God." (Ephesians 3:16-21)

2. **Christ's Divine Power Supplies Everything We Need**
   Consider *"Seeing that His divine power has granted to us everything pertaining to life and godliness, through the true knowledge of Him who called us by His own glory and excellence." (2 Peter 1:3)*

   This verse dismantles the idea that we must generate our own godliness. Everything needed for life and godliness has already been given to us in Christ. The key is not self-effort but a growing knowledge of Him. As we abide in Him, we progressively experience the fullness of His divine power working in and flowing out of us.

3. **Eternal Life Is Not Just a Destination—It Is a Person**
   Many view eternal life as simply living forever in heaven. But Jesus defines eternal life differently—it is not just about duration but about relationship. *"This is eternal life, that they may know You, the only true God, and Jesus Christ whom You have sent." (John 17:3)* To have eternal life is to know Christ intimately. The more we grasp this, the more we move from striving to abiding, from self-effort to trust, from religious activity to a spiritual relationship.

4. **The Reign of Christ's Life Supersedes the Reign of Sin**
   Sin once ruled over us, leading to death. But in Christ, grace reigns through His righteousness, bringing eternal life. This is not a self-generated righteousness but a righteousness that comes from Christ Himself. *"So that, as sin reigned in death, even so grace would reign through righteousness to eternal life through Jesus Christ our Lord." (Romans 5:21).*

5. **The Gift of Eternal Life in Christ**
   "For the wages of sin is death, but the free gift of God is eternal life in Christ Jesus our Lord." (Romans 6:23). This well-known verse highlights the contrast between self-effort and divine grace. Sin's wages bring death, but eternal life is a free gift. The Christian life is never a wage we earn—it is a gift we receive and manifest.

6. **Christ's Indwelling Power Transforms Our Mortal Lives**
   "But if the Spirit of Him who raised Jesus from the dead dwells in you, He who raised Christ Jesus from the dead will also give life to your mortal bodies through His Spirit who dwells in you." (Romans 8:11). This is a profound reality: The same Spirit who raised Christ from the dead is at work in us. This means that Christian living is not about self-discipline alone but about resurrection power alive in us. We have been given everything in Christ.

The Difference Between Being Like Jesus (Imitation) and Christ Indwelling Life

Trying to Be Like Jesus	**Christ Living Through Us**
Based on self-effort	Based on yielding to the Spirit
Striving for holiness	Receiving holiness by abiding in Christ
Focused on personal discipline	Focused on spiritual dependence
Outward behavior modification	Inward growth by the Spirit

The Christian life is not about trying harder but dying more completely.

Key Warnings of only "Being like Jesus"
(doing the activities of Jesus without His life and power)

Jesus condemned those who were religious and did the things of God yet did not have a new heart. *Matthew 7:21-23 – "Not everyone who says to me, 'Lord, Lord,' will enter the kingdom of heaven, but the one who does the will of my Father who is in heaven. On that day many will say to me, 'Lord, Lord, did we not prophesy in your name, and cast out demons in your name, and do many mighty works in your name?' And then will I declare to them, 'I never knew you; depart from me, you workers of lawlessness.'"*

Works in His name alone are not what changes a life. This warning echoes Jesus' rebuke of the Pharisees: *Matthew 23:27-28 – "Whitewashed tombs" that look clean on the outside but are full of hypocrisy.*

Appearance only is condemned. *2 Timothy 3:1-5, "But understand this, that in the last days there will come times of difficulty. For people will be lovers of self, lovers of money, proud, arrogant, abusive, disobedient to their parents, ungrateful, unholy, heartless, unappeasable, slanderous, without self-control, brutal, not loving good, treacherous, reckless, swollen with conceit, lovers of pleasure rather than lovers of God, having the appearance of godliness, but denying its power. Avoid such people."*

1 Samuel 16:7 "But the Lord said to Samuel, 'Do not look on his appearance or on the height of his stature, because I have rejected him. For the Lord sees not as man sees: man looks on the outward appearance, but the Lord looks on the heart.'"

The prophet Samuel was sent to anoint a new king after Saul's failure. He saw Eliab, one of Jesse's sons, and assumed he was God's choice because of his impressive outward appearance. But God corrected Samuel, showing that divine selection is based on the heart, not external traits. David, the youngest and least expected son, was chosen instead because of his heart for God.

The Exchanged Life: Crucifying the Flesh for Christ's Fullness

The cross is not only where Jesus died for us, but it is also where we died with Him. When we truly grasp that our old self is dead and that Christ Himself is our life, we enter into what has been called "the exchanged life." Our old self was crucified with Christ, meaning that we no longer live by our own strength but by His life within us.

The cross is not only where Jesus died for you; it is where you died with Him. Your old self is dead; now, Christ is your very life.

Galatians 5:16 – "But I say, walk by the Spirit, and you will not gratify the desires of the flesh."

Galatians 5:18 – "But if you are led by the Spirit, you are not under the law."

Galatians 5:25 – "If we live by the Spirit, let us also keep in step with the Spirit."

Application: The Pathway to Experience Christ as Our Life

How Do We Do This? Recognize Your Own Powerlessness – Until we acknowledge that we cannot live the Christian life in our strength, we will never experience His power.

Instead of exhausting ourselves trying to be like Jesus, we must realize that Christ is our life. Our role is not to strive but to abandon, not to imitate but to be intimate. This is the secret to the Christian life: Christ in you, the hope of glory (Colossians 1:27). It is not about trying harder, but about trusting deeper. When we grasp this, we will finally experience the fullness of the abundant life He promised.

What do we do? *"Quit trying to be like Jesus you will never be perfect"*.

Shift in three primary ways.

Surrender *"if anyone wished to come after me, let Him deny himself, take up his cross and follow me."* Luke 9:23 Surrender is dying to self—

not just to sin, but to self-effort, self-glory, and self-dependence. It is not about trying harder, but letting go.

Appropriate Appropriation is actively laying hold of what's already ours in Christ. He is the source of life, power, and wisdom. We draw from Him as our source as our roots go deeper. Our will power does not bring lasting change, God's will and His power does. *2 Corinthians 12:9, "My grace is sufficient power is perfected in weakness."*

Be Led by the Spirit "For all who are led by the Spirit of God are sons of God." Romans 8:14 The Spirit is the one who makes Christ's life real and active within us.

The Implications of Christ as Our Life

When Christ is truly our life, our entire perspective shifts:

> **From Imitation to Indwelling Spirit** – We no longer try to "act like Jesus." He transforms us from the inside out (Colossians 3:4).
> **From Duty to Delight** – Christianity is no longer about trying to please God out of obligation but experiencing Him in love and joy.
> **From Self-Effort to Rest** – Instead of striving to be spiritual, we rest in Christ's sufficiency and His work in us.
> **From Temporal to Eternal Perspective** – We no longer live for ourselves but for His kingdom, with God's purposes and priorities shaping our daily decisions.

The Yielded Life of Major W. Ian Thomas - A life Story of Trying to Be Like Jesus to Letting Jesus Live Through You

In the early years of his Christian life, Major W. Ian Thomas was the kind of believer many looked up to. Bright, passionate, articulate, and disciplined—he was a young man fully devoted to the cause of Christ. By age 19, he was already a seasoned evangelist, preaching five to six times a week, leading Bible studies, and passionately laboring to bring others to Christ. He was admired for his zeal, his knowledge, and his unwavering commitment. And yet, behind all of that ministry activity, Ian Thomas was utterly exhausted.

Inwardly, his soul was growing dry. Though externally active and effective, he felt spiritually depleted, hollow, and increasingly desperate. He was doing everything he knew to do for Jesus—but it wasn't enough. Not enough to produce rest. Not enough to give joy. Not enough to feel alive. Like many sincere believers, he was unknowingly living out of *Romans 7:18 "For I have the desire to do what is good, but I cannot carry it out"*. He was trying to be like Jesus but finding that he couldn't sustain it. That crisis came to a head one night after another full day of Christian activity. He returned home late, fell to his knees beside his bed, and said these unforgettable words to God:

"Lord Jesus, I am so fed up with this Christian life I am living. I am trying my best, I am giving everything I've got, and yet I am so empty, so powerless, so dry. If this is what the Christian life is, I'm done with it." At that moment, something broke. And God spoke—not audibly, but with unmistakable clarity: *"You have been trying to live for Me on your terms, in your strength. But I never said I would help you live for Me. I said I would live My life through you."*

In that moment, Ian Thomas quit. He stopped trying to be like Jesus and started trusting Christ to live in him and through him. It was his *white funeral*—the death of self-effort and the birth of true life. Galatians 2:20 suddenly became real: *"I have been crucified with Christ and I no longer live, but Christ lives in me."* This would change everything.

The End of Trying, the Beginning of Trusting

What Ian Thomas discovered in his brokenness is the same truth we must all come to grips with: we cannot live the Christian life. Only Jesus can live His life in and through us. Our best efforts, regardless how sincere, will eventually fail. Why? Because God never designed us to imitate Christ in our strength—but to *appropriate* Christ in dying.

Thomas began teaching that the Christian life is not a self-improvement project but a supernatural exchange: our weakness for His strength, our inability for His sufficiency, our striving for His indwelling. He would often say:

"*The Christian life is nothing less than the life which He lived then... lived now by Him in you.*" This truth freed him. He no longer lived under the crushing burden of performance. Ministry became an overflow, not an obligation. Fruitfulness emerged, not from pushing harder, but from abiding deeper. He was no longer the source—Christ was.

The Shift We All Must Make

Change doesn't come by trying harder. It comes by being renewed in our minds—specifically, in how we understand the Christian life. We do not become like Jesus by mimicking Him. We become like Him by *yielding* to Him.

This is the great paradox of the Christian life: victory comes through surrender, power through dependence, and fruitfulness through abiding. When we live that way, the burden lifts, and the life of Christ begins to flow like living water.

Reflection: The End of Me, the Beginning of Him

Are you exhausted from trying to be like Jesus? Are you dry from years of effort and performance? Are you admired by others, but inwardly frustrated and empty?

The Glove and the Hand

A glove, by itself, is lifeless. It cannot move, grasp, or accomplish anything. But when a hand enters the glove, the glove takes on the life of the hand—it moves, acts, and functions, not by its own power, but by the life within it. This is the picture of the Christian life. We are like gloves—powerless on our own—but when Christ fills us, we live with His life, His power, and His purpose.

Conclusion: Quit Trying and Start Trusting

Many believers live exhausted, frustrated, and defeated because they are trying to "be like Jesus" instead of allowing Him to live through them. The reality of the transformed Christian life is not about imitation but incarnation—*"Christ in you, the hope of glory" (Colossians 1:27).*

Instead of trying harder, give up. Instead of striving, rest. Instead of doing for God, let Him work through you. This is the key to experiencing the abundant, victorious Christian life.

Shift #1 Summary: Christlike → Christ Life (WHO)

- From imitation to indwelling.
- Application: surrender, appropriation, Spirit-led life.

Core Idea: The Christian life is not imitation but incarnation—Christ living His life through you.

Practical Steps

1. Surrender Daily – Begin each morning releasing control: "Jesus, live Your life through me."
2. Appropriate His Promises – Anchor in one verse (Gal. 2:20, Col. 3:4) and claim it in your circumstances.
3. Be Spirit-Led in Decisions – Pause before acting: "Am I striving, or abiding?"
4. Replace Effort with Rest – Lay down one self-driven activity and invite Christ to work through you.
5. Reflect & Record – Journal moments of striving vs. depending on Christ.

Reflection Questions

- Where am I still trying to imitate Jesus instead of letting Him live through me?

- What areas of my life show more striving than surrender?
- How would my day look different if I truly believed Christ was my source of strength?
- What is one step of surrender I can take this week?

SHIFT #1 CHRIST LIKE TO CHRIST LIFE   WHO?

Chapter Five

Shift #2
For Christ to From Christ
WHY?

"Take care of the depth of your walk, and God will take care of the breadth of your impact." — **Walt Henrichsen**

"But as for me, the nearness of God is my good, the Lord God is my refuge, that I tell of all your work." — **Psalm 73:28**

Living from Christ

Often in our Christian walk we can get the mission and our activity ahead of our relationship with Christ. This leads to burnout and valuing the accomplishments more than the people. This is especially prevalent with anyone who is in vocational ministry or is a pastor in a church. It is the cause of many marriages and families of Christian workers suffering and even falling apart.

The second shift which is to move from trying to do things for the Lord and abide to do things from Him embraces the condition of our relationship with Christ, our sensitivity to know God's will and our purpose as well as a deep introspection of our motives and feelings—things that often drive us ahead of the Lord."

John McCue – From Chaos to Christ, From Wash Bay to Leadership

The life story of my friend, John McCue, is a great picture of how the Lord intervenes and works in a life to bring it from challenges to a sense of purpose and meaning that has great impact. The Lord restores a life in order to flow through it.

"I've made it 48 years, but looking back, I see the hand of God and His purposes in every chapter.

A Childhood Marked by Brokenness

I was born into a young marriage that was already fragile. My father, an MP in the military, battled alcoholism and rage. He carried deep wounds himself — having watched his own father killed by a drunk driver. But his pain spilled over into abuse toward my mom, my brother, and me. When I was around seven, my mom finally left. My father walked out soon after, and his presence in my life faded.

From then on, instability became normal. We bounced between grandparents, apartments, and eventually life with a stepfather. I was angry, volatile, and often violent. Twice I was even institutionalized in mental hospitals because no one knew what to do with me. Though my grandmother tried to root me in faith through the Catholic Church, I didn't understand. I only felt abandoned and ashamed.

Meeting Keisha – God's Instrument of Grace

As a teenager, I poured my frustration into punk music — tattoos, mohawks, angry songs — and into fights. Then God sent me a gift I didn't deserve: Keisha. She came from a wealthy family, but what stood out wasn't money — it was her faith, her compassion, and the way she looked at me and said, "You're not a bad guy."

Our first night together wasn't about rebellion; it was about conversation. The next morning, she took me to Southeast Christian Church in Louisville. I didn't get saved that day, but something shifted. For the first time, someone cared enough to see past the chaos in me.

Fatherhood and Faith

When Keisha and I had our daughter, reality hit. Holding that tiny baby, I realized I couldn't keep living selfishly. This child hadn't asked to be born — and it was my responsibility to protect and provide. That was the beginning of real change. Over the years, I wrestled with doubt. I was baptized multiple times, sometimes questioning if I was "really saved." But slowly, through my wife's faith and the Word of God, I began to see that salvation is not about my performance — it's about Christ's finished work.

A Journey Through Work and Leadership

I started at Sodrel Trucking at the bottom — washing buses, fixing engines, driving trucks. I worked every position but accounting. Today, I help oversee this multimillion-dollar company with 400 employees. But what grounds me isn't business strategy — it's Scripture.

The Bible has become my leadership manual. God is a God of order, not chaos. His Word teaches how to lead: with truth, with compassion, and with humility. Christ washing His disciples' feet shows me that leadership means serving others, not lording over them.

Perspective

I still battle my ADHD, and I've had labels like "bipolar" thrown at me. But I've learned that faith in Christ reframes even my struggles. Structure, once my enemy, has become my protection. And when trials come — as they always do — I remember: every great figure in the Bible faced tribulations before God used them mightily. Today, my life is evidence that God can take a broken, angry, abandoned boy and turn him into a man who leads, provides, and points others toward truth.

Invitation

If my story says anything, it's this: you don't have to stay stuck in your past. Facts are stubborn things, and the greatest fact of all is the cross. Christ changes everything. Yielding to Him is the only way chaos becomes order, despair becomes hope, and brokenness becomes a testimony.

Shift the Focus of Doing for Christ to Doing from Christ

John 15:4–5, "Abide in Me, and I in you. As the branch cannot bear fruit of itself unless it abides in the vine, so neither can you unless you abide in Me. I am the vine, you are the branches; he who abides in Me and I in him, he bears much fruit, for apart from Me you can do nothing."

This passage captures the second shift every believer must make: from striving by doing things *for* Christ, to allowing Christ to live and work through us. It's not a call to passivity, but to a relationship so alive that His life naturally produces a harvest.

Three Observations from the Vine

1. **The Branch Abides** – A branch's only responsibility is to remain connected to the vine. "Abide" means to dwell, to be at home, to rest. It is not hurried busyness for God, but steady, personal depth with Him. Imagine a grapevine in late summer. The branch doesn't wake up and "decide" to push out grapes—it simply stays connected, and the life of the vine does the work. When we focus on abiding instead of producing, we are freed from comparison, pride, and discouragement. Life becomes the overflow of love.

   We grow by remaining in Christ—drawing life from His Word, walking in obedience, and dying to self. Ministry to the Lord comes before ministry for the Lord.

2. **The Branch Carries Life** – Christ is the vine; we are the branches. The vine supplies life, the branch carries it. We are not the source of spiritual life or power—only the channel. A garden hose doesn't manufacture water; it simply carries it from the source to the destination. In the same way, we are conduits of His life. We are not independent workers for God but vessels through which Christ works. Our prayer shifts from "Lord, help me do this" to "Lord, live this through me."

   Philippians 1:21 "For me to live is Christ."

Colossians 3:3-4 – *"For you have died, and your life is hidden with Christ in God. When Christ, who is our life, is revealed, then you also will be revealed with Him in glory."*

3. **The Branch Bears Fruit** – The branch does not produce fruit; it bears the fruit that the vine produces. We cannot manufacture spiritual outcomes; they are the result of Christ's life at work in us. Fruitfulness is the natural overflow of abiding, not the product of self-effort. The fruit of the Spirit (Galatians 5:22–23) flows from His life, not our labor. Bearing a harvest is the mark of a true disciple.

    Character – the fruit of the Spirit in daily life (Galatians 5:22–23)
    Conduct – righteousness (Philippians 1:11)
    Participation – making disciples (Matthew 28:19–20)

Why This Shift is Important

Many Christians and ministries operate as though the Christian life is about doing things *for* God—paying Him back, proving our worth, or pursuing our own plans with His blessing. But John 15 reveals the opposite: we are made for His purposes, not ours.

Warning: Proverbs 16:3 and Psalm 37:4 are often twisted into "If my plan is good and I love God; He will make it happen." This is not biblical.

Ken Boa insight: God's love is "causeless, measureless, and ceaseless." We cannot make Him love us more or less. We minister from His love, not to earn it.

When we reverse the order—trying to serve before we rest—we risk self-reliance, burnout, and ministry. We may even see visible "results" while being spiritually empty.

The Warning and the Call

The greatest danger in Christian service is when the work of God begins to replace our relationship with God. While we are indeed called to make a difference, this must be the natural overflow of a thriving, intimate connection with Christ—not the result of our personal ambition, drive, or ministry strategies.

Spiritual deceptions occurs when we allow our purpose to overshadow Christ. We were created to glorify God (Isa. 43:7), yet in the pursuit of that purpose, we can become so driven that we put the mission ahead of people and ahead of our own relationship with the Lord. In this distorted mindset, success becomes measured by visible outcomes—numbers, impact, influence—rather than the inward reality of knowing and enjoying Christ.

Another danger is when we focus more on the fruit than on abiding in the Vine. Many believers find themselves obsessed with the results— how much they know, how much influence they have or how effectively they are "advancing the kingdom." We become fruit inspectors, evaluating our own worth or the worth of others based on perceived productivity. This leads to either pride or despair—pride when the outcome appears abundant, despair when it seems lacking.

The ultimate warning in this passage is that a branch disconnected from the vine withers (John 15:6). It may still look healthy for a time, just as many leaders appear successful outwardly while inwardly, they are spiritually dry. But eventually, separation from Christ results in lifelessness. This is why Jesus repeatedly calls His disciples to abide, remain, and stay connected to Him.

Thus, the greatest priority in the Christian life is not effort, effectiveness, or results—it is Christ Himself. Before we seek to accomplish anything for Him, we must first seek to know Him, love Him, and be transformed by Him. As we do, the change will come, not by our striving but by His life manifested in us.

The Call: Quit trying to do things *for* Christ. Let Him do His work *through* you. Be in union with Him—rest, renew, remain. When you do, the evidence of Christ will come, and it will last.

Knowing our Purpose is absolutely critical, otherwise we confuse being "driven" with being called.

This strikes at the heart of shifting from for to from. Doing things "for" the Lord speaks more to our drivenness because it puts us central. Whereas "from" inherently has Christ at the center which is what calling is all about. Calling has three levels: first, we are called to Him, second, we are called to His purposes, and third, we are called to a context where we live out this relationship.

Consider the writings of Gordon Macdonald. He lists some of these symptoms.

1. *Driven people are most often only gratified by accomplishments and symbols of achievement. Badges, titles, positions, status. The more stuff on the wall, the better the GPA, the more pages on the resume, the better the driven person feels—at least until they discover someone who has more.*

2. *Driven people are caught up in the uncontrolled pursuit of expansion. Driven people aren't satisfied with the status quo. In a sense, that's not a bad thing. At the same time, growing a business or a church at all costs can leave lots of casualties in our wake. Driven people tend to like to build their own kingdoms at the expense of others.*

3. *Driven people often have a limited regard for integrity. Speed and efficiency can lead to cutting corners. Driven people can easily justify making poor ethical choices in order to achieve their ends.*

4. *Driven people are not likely to bother themselves with the honing of people skills. Driven people tend to use people as a means to an end, rather than seeing them as individuals worthy of attention and love.*

5. *Driven people tend to be highly competitive. Yup. It's not enough to compete. You have to win. Driven people see second place as being the first loser. For me to go home after losing a softball game and not replay it over and over again all night is a major victory for me!*

6. *Driven people often possess a volcanic force of anger. Driven people don't take criticism well because it challenges their perfectionism. Criticism about something we have done gets translated into a value judgment on us as a person. Driven people tend to respond to an attack with overwhelming emotional firepower.*

7. *Driven people are usually abnormally busy, are averse to play, and usually avoid spiritual worship. We need to guard against losing our soul by neglecting reading the Bible, prayer, and quiet time.*

Driven people usually end up like Saul—falling on their own swords, exhausting themselves and others. The truth is that driven people will never enjoy the tranquility of an ordered private world without a new vision for their lives. Overcoming driven-ness requires some brutal honesty about ourselves. We must be able to forgive ourselves and others for becoming this way. We must be able to slow down, to make time for our souls to catch up with our bodies.

To do that we must learn that there is an alternative to the driven life. MacDonald rightly names this the "called" life. His biblical example is John the Baptist. Interestingly, John is the one biblical character that most people want to skip over in the Gospels in order to get to Jesus.

John the Baptist gives us a window into what this "called life" looks like:

1. *Called people understand stewardship. John realized that the crowds that were coming out to hear him preach were never his in the first place. God had placed them under his care for a period of time and had taken them back when Jesus came on the scene. John didn't really own anything in his life, which left him free to see everything as belonging to God.*

2. *Called people know exactly who they are. John was clear in telling the crowds who he was not. He was not the Messiah. Defining who we are not is really the first step in knowing who we are. John didn't believe his own press...he believed God. He not only knew who he*

was but who he really belonged to. Knowing who we are takes some deep reflection. We are never as good or as bad as we think people see us. Called people define themselves according to their relationship with God, valuing God's love and grace-filled approval over any amount of applause.

3. *Called people possess an unwavering sense of purpose.* John used the metaphor of a wedding to describe his role. The coming messiah was to be the groom that everyone was waiting for. John was simply the best man. The best man helps with the preparations, but when the groom appears he stands off to the side and says nothing, focusing all the attention on the bride and groom. When the crowd headed toward Jesus, John had no sense of jealousy. He had done his job well. Called people do a lot more listening than talking…a lot more reflecting than pontificating. Called people choose their time and priorities according to their purpose.

4. *Called people practice unswerving commitment.* But don't believe the self-aggrandizing propaganda that there is no one who can replace you; the organization cannot do without you. Do well and be willing to let go.

When you examine your life, what does the motivation gauge read? Are you called or are you driven?

Application: John 15:5 – Growing in Abiding Intimacy with Christ

1. **Abide in Relationship**

   The foundation of a fruitful life is abiding in Christ. Jesus said, *"I am the vine; you are the branches. Whoever abides in me and I in him, he it is that bears much fruit, for apart from me you can do nothing"* (John 15:5). This is not an invitation to strive, but a call to remain and rest. Abiding means cultivating a deep love with Christ—knowing Him, walking with Him, and being nourished by His presence daily.

Christ's love makes us whole. His love heals the wounds of performance-based acceptance and striving (John 13:34-35).

Spiritual growth comes as we apply His Word. Jesus said, *"If you abide in my word, you are truly my disciples" (John 8:31).*

Worship strengthens our connection. Worship aligns our hearts with the truth that He is the source of all life *(Romans 8:28-29).*

2. **Rest – Let Go & Cease Striving Dependence**
    Many believers live as though their success or significance depends on their effort. But Jesus calls us to let go, cease striving, and trust Him.

Be thankful in all things (1 Thessalonians 5:18). Gratitude shifts our perspective from what we can do to what He is doing

Trust that He is in control (Romans 8:38-39). Abiding means resting—acknowledging that Christ is the One producing harvest in us, not our own efforts. Hudson Taylor on the abiding life: *"I used to ask God to help me. Then I asked if I might help Him. I ended up by asking Him to do His work in and through me."* Let go of self-effort and let Christ work through you.

3. **Be a Conduit for Fruit-Bearing**
    Jesus produces growth through us as we yield to Him. The fruit of the Spirit is not something we manufacture but something He cultivates in us (Galatians 5:22-23).

Be a vessel, not the source. The branch does not strain to bear fruit—it simply remains connected to the vine. Pursue purity and obedience. Sin and self-reliance obstruct the flow of His life in us. Jesus said, *"You are already clean because of the word I have spoken to you" (John 15:3).* Stay in that purity through confession, obedience, and humility.

C. S. Lewis: From Self-Sufficiency to Abiding in Christ

Clive Staples Lewis, life story fully reflects this intimate relationship. He was known to the world as C. S. Lewis, began life with a vivid imagination and a stubborn independence. Born in Belfast in 1898, he grew up devouring books and creating fantasy worlds with his brother Warnie. When his mother died of cancer at just nine years old, young Lewis learned to retreat inward. His father, unable to bridge the emotional gap, left him feeling alone. In that loneliness, Lewis cultivated two things that would shape his life: a fierce reliance on his own intellect and an insatiable longing for joy that this world could never fully satisfy.

As he moved through school and into Oxford, his sharp mind grew into an armor. War in the trenches of France during World War I hardened his skepticism further, and by his early twenties, Lewis had cast off the idea of God altogether. He pursued brilliance, high standards, and reason as if life depended on what he could do for himself. Faith, he believed, was for the weak. He would strive, succeed, and live by his own efforts.

Yet Lewis could not silence the longing that haunted him. In literature, beauty, and myth, he felt what he called "stabs of joy"—moments of piercing delight that pointed beyond the world. The irony was not lost on him: the very myths he studied seemed to whisper of a greater Story. His intellectual striving, his "for-myself" living, could never deliver the peace or satisfaction he craved.

The turning point came not by his own striving, but by friendship. J. R. R. Tolkien and Hugo Dyson patiently walked with him, not urging him to do something *for* Christ, but to see that Christ had already done everything for him. Christianity was not a system to imitate, but a life to accept. One late night in 1931, after hours of honest talk, Lewis recognized what he had resisted all along: *"I gave in and admitted that God was God."* Shortly after, he yielded to Christ Himself—not as an example to copy, but as the Living Vine into whom he must live.

From that letting go, Lewis's life was transformed. He did not suddenly set out to "work for God" in his own strength. Instead, his writing, teaching, and imagination became channels through which Christ's life flowed. In *Mere Christianity* he explained faith with clarity that spoke to millions—not because he forced himself to produce, but because Christ was producing fruit through him. In *The Chronicles of Narnia*, he opened a window to the wonder of the gospel—Aslan breathing life into a frozen world—reflecting the reality he himself had discovered: that apart from Christ, there is nothing, but abiding in Him brings life.

Even in sorrow—losing his beloved wife, Joy, to cancer—Lewis learned that abiding meant trusting, even through grief. His journal of lament, *A Grief Observed*, did not emerge from self-strength but from Christ's sustaining presence when all else fell apart.

When Lewis died in 1963, his legacy was not of a man who did great things *for* Christ, but of one through whom Christ worked. His life illustrates the truth he finally embraced: the Christian life is not self-effort but union. For apart from Him, we can do nothing—but abiding in Him, even the most ordinary man can bear eternal harvest.

C. S. Lewis Mere Christianity: *"Your real, new self (which is Christ's and also yours, and yours just because it is His) will not come as long as you are looking for it. It will come when you are looking for Him….Give up yourself. And you will find your real self. Lose your life and you will save it…. Keep back nothing. Nothing that you have not given away will ever be really yours. Nothing in you that has not died will ever be raised from the dead. Look for yourself and you will find in the long run only hatred, loneliness, despair, rage, ruin, and decay. But look for Christ and you will find Him, and with Him everything else will be thrown in."*

Conclusion: Quit Trying to Work for Jesus—He doesn't need you. Let Him Work in and Through You.

Jesus does not need you to work for Him, but He wants to work through you. He does not call us to *perform* for Him but to *remain* in Him. We are unconditionally loved, not because of what we do, but because of who He is. The branch does not strive; it simply rests.

Stop trying to do things for Christ.
Stop striving to manufacture spiritual outcomes.
Stop measuring your worth by what you accomplish.

Instead, rest in His love, walk in His Word, receive His Spirit, and let His life flow through you. The only way to make a difference is to be at home in Him. Will you die to your self-effort today and commit to living from Christ, not for Christ?

Shift #2 Summary: For Christ → From Christ (WHY)

- Abiding as the foundation of ministry.
- Danger of drivenness vs. the freedom of calling.

Core Idea: Ministry and life should flow from intimacy with Christ, not frantic doing for Him.

Practical Steps
1. Abide First – Schedule time with Christ before engaging in tasks.
2. Shift Your Prayer Language – Replace "Lord, help me" with "Lord, live this through me."
3. Check Motives – Ask: "Am I serving to prove myself, or out of overflow from Christ?"
4. Guard Relationships – Prioritize presence with God and family over activity.
5. Weekly Reset – Review where you drifted into "for" instead of "from" and recalibrate

Reflection Questions
- Do I find more identity in what I do for God than who I am in Him?
- When was the last time I served from overflow instead of out of obligation?
- What activities or ministries may have replaced intimacy with Christ in my schedule?
- How can I re-center my motives on abiding instead of proving?

SHIFT #2   FOR CHRIST TO FROM CHRIST   WHY?

Chapter Six

Shift #3
Achieve to Receive
WHAT?

"Hold everything in your hands lightly, otherwise it hurts when God pries your fingers open."
— **Corrie ten Boom, Nazi Holocaust survivor**

"Therefore, as you have received Christ Jesus the Lord, so walk in Him, having been firmly rooted and now being built up in Him and established in your faith, just as you were instructed and overflowing with gratitude." — **Colossians 2:6-7**

Moving from Effort to Gift

We live in a world that applauds and rewards accomplishment. We find this in sports the winners are exalted, and losers are forgotten. Education exalts the top of the class while everybody else is left behind. The business world is always looking for winners and not people that come in second place. The list could go on

The great tragedy in our time is we've applied this achievement mentality to Christianity both in terms of our walk with the Lord but also in terms of what we produce for the Lord. So why do we do this? The world is based on a performance-based acceptance mentality and with this comes but it is also underlying perspective of gaining our identity by what we get done or what people think of us.

In the Christian life it is totally opposite our position in Jesus Christ alone, it is not based on works but it's based on grace and mercy both of which we did not deserve. This becomes the basis for our third foundational shift which is to move from achieving to receiving. We must take hold of the gifts, the promises, and the love of God fully. And as we take hold of these infinite resources they multiply as we give them away people in need.

My dear friend, Trey Miller, shares his life story that reflects this shift.

Trey Miller: From Abandonment to Abiding – A Story of Redemption

I was born in Atlanta, Georgia, in 1969, the youngest of three children. At six months old, my mother moved us to St. Louis to be near family. My father helped with the move but chose not to return with us. That was it—he abandoned us.

Growing up in St. Louis, I lived in a small apartment with two older sisters and a mother doing her best. When she remarried, we became a blended family of five children. For a while, it seemed like stability had come, but at 13 my mom divorced again. Overwhelmed, she sent my younger brother to live with his dad, and I was sent to mine in Columbus, Georgia. The back-and-forth continued, disrupting school, friendships, and my sense of belonging. By my senior year, I dropped out.

My grandfather took me in, helped me earn my GED, and encouraged college. But I lacked the study habits and vision to succeed. I drifted through my twenties—jobs, apartments, survival. Outwardly moving forward, but inwardly empty.

Yet God never stopped pursuing me.

In October 1986, at a church revival while living with my father, the gospel broke through. At 16, I gave my life to Christ. For a season, I read the Bible and prayed, but with no discipleship the fire faded. The next decade became a tug-of-war between who I knew I could be and who I settled for.

In 1999, hungry for something more, I accepted an invitation back to church. This time it wasn't curiosity—it was desperation. That year I rededicated my life to Christ, choosing to live full-on for Him. Soon after, I joined a Bible study led by Ken Boa at the Piedmont Center. That group changed everything. For the first time, I was discipled. I learned that following Jesus wasn't about striving but abiding—allowing Him to live His life through me.

Not long after, I met my wife, Marjorie. We came from different backgrounds, but our shared love for Christ became our foundation. We raised three daughters, pouring Scripture and prayer into their lives as my mentor had poured into me. Marriage and parenting weren't without struggles—different styles, financial stress, and Marjorie's health challenges—but God used those hardships to knit us together. Grace became the glue of our family.

Over time, I discovered that walking with Jesus is not a checklist but a continual conversation. He's not confined to morning devotions; He's in every thought, every reaction, every breath. That intimacy has sustained me, especially in the past year, when I lost my father, my mother, and our home to fire. Three crushing blows. Yet beneath the grief, I experienced what Philippians calls "the peace that transcends all understanding."

When people ask, "How are you still standing?" my answer is simple: 100% Jesus. His Spirit in me. His grace around me. His provision sustaining me.

My story isn't about resilience—it's about redemption. About a Savior who never gave up on me, even when I gave up on myself. About a Father who never left, even when my earthly one did.

I don't know what tomorrow holds. But I know who holds me. And that's enough.

The Achievement Mentality

In the world's way of thinking, achievement is often measured by what we can see, count, and celebrate. We focus on outcomes—accomplishing tasks, producing results, making things happen—and we want them now.

SHIFT #3 ACHIEVE TO RECEIVE   WHAT?

Tangible progress feels satisfying because it's measurable; we can track goals, tally wins, and keep score. This can drive us to great effort, but it also tempts us to grip our goals too tightly, as if the metric defines us. We crave neatness, order, and visible success. We prefer a life without problems, and we guard our image to maintain the appearance of having it all together. Without realizing it, we begin to reflect the world's obsession with winners and losers, forgetting that God's measures are different from man's.

The achievement mentality also fuels our desire for control. We subtly take on the role of playing God, assuming we can manage outcomes and make something happen. The flesh thrives on control because it gives a false sense of security—if we can orchestrate the details, we feel safe. But life resists such control. It is full of ups and downs, and how fast we run or how hard we push, we cannot outrun our problems. Control is a mirage, and pursuing it drains us of peace.

Tied closely to accomplishment is the way it affects our sense of self-worth. In Christ, our true significance is secure—we are already loved, already chosen. But when production defines us, we begin to seek worth through comparison and competition. We count wins, stack accomplishments, and evaluate ourselves against others. The flesh loves to measure because it gives a sense of identity—but it's fragile, always vulnerable to the next loss or failure. Contentment comes only when we shift to being satisfied with doing our very best as unto the Lord, rather than striving to be the best in the world's eyes.

Perhaps the most subtle and dangerous form of achievement mentality is performance-based acceptance. The world runs on it—in education, sports, business, and even parenting—and it conditions us to believe that value is earned through performance. Without realizing it, we import this mindset into our spiritual life. We can turn evangelism, discipleship, Bible study, and even prayer into performance-driven activities. We approach prayer as if the goal is to get something done—moving God, proving devotion—rather than abiding in relationship with Him. The irony is that in striving to "do for God," we can drift from truly being with Him.

The challenges with this mindset are many. First, God produces the harvest, not us. We can work all day and have little to show for it if we are operating apart from His power. Second, His timing and ways rarely match ours; impatience is the enemy of abiding. Third, worldly results are temporary—they will not survive the fire of eternity. Fourth, the idea that "the end justifies the means" is foreign to the kingdom of God; with Him, the ends and the means both are important. And finally, the only things we truly control are our motives, our faithfulness, our attitude, and our effort. The rest belongs to Him.

The Dangers of an Achievement Mentality

You will never stay on top. There is always a faster gun in town. If you arrive you will never stay, there

Accomplishment perspective implies we are needed and central to God's work. Accomplishment gives us significance, lifts us up.

Outcome focus equates the product as a sign of our level of maturity

Gain mindset says that how hard you work directly correlates to how much you produce

Validation of our work is found in the outcome and gives us significance, proves our self-worth

Legalism can be a by-product of a production perspective – focus on image rather than the heart.

All of this leads to Pride, Competing and Comparing.

An achievement mindset leads us to be constantly "Measuring the Work of God".

"*This is like holding onto water. With the work of God, you will never be able to determine success by that which you measure, and comparing yourself with others is at best, counterproductive. For we are not bold to class or compare ourselves with some of those who commend themselves; but when they measure themselves by themselves and compare themselves with themselves, they are without understanding. 2 Corinthians 10:12*" May 9th Entry from Thoughts from *The Diary of a Desperate Man: A Daily Devotional* by Walter A Henrichsen

Illustration – The Cup 2 Views

Take a cup. Is it empty or full? With natural eyes, it looks empty. But in truth, it is full of air—like the Holy Spirit. The question is: are we looking with spiritual eyes or natural ones?

Now take a cup half-filled with water. Is it half-empty or half-full? A success mentality sees the empty half and says, "There's more to do—we haven't done enough." A receiving mentality sees the full half and thanks God for what has already been given

The Receiving Mentality

Where the success mentality looks to human effort, the receiving mentality rests in the truth that God *gives*. He is a generous Father who delights to bless His children—not as a reward for performance, but as a gift of grace. Scripture tells us that *"in Christ we have been blessed with every spiritual blessing "(Ephesians 1:3)*. We have been given a new nature and a new family. These gifts redefine everything about us. They are not earned; they are received. And they are always for our good, meeting every true need in His perfect timing and way.

The gifts God gives are abundant and varied: eternal life, spiritual life, forgiveness, grace, truth, spiritual gifts, talents, strengths, relationships, and the promises of His Word. They meet our deepest longings for acceptance, significance, belonging, and well-being. As Peter writes, *"His divine power has granted to us everything pertaining to life and godliness"* (2 Peter 1:3). Our role is not to strive for what we lack, but to accept what He has already given—and to do so with gratitude rather than presumption.

Receiving Requires Faith and Humility

Receiving is not passive—it is an active expression of faith and humility. It acknowledges that apart from Christ, we can produce nothing of eternal value. To accept from Him, we must let go of our tight grip on the world's goods and release our dependence on our own performance. Open hands are a sign of trust—trust that God will give what is needed when it is needed.

Sometimes what He gives is immediate and tangible; other times it is unseen and future—grace for the present moment, peace that guards the heart, or rewards that will only be revealed in heaven. Gratitude is the language of faith. When we thank Him for what He has given, we affirm our trust in His goodness, even when we cannot yet see the outcome.

Receiving Requires Presence

One of the greatest enemies of a receiving mentality is distraction. Work, ministry, and the drive to succeed can subtly draw our attention away from the Lord who is the source of life. Receiving requires that we slow down, pay attention, and be present with Him. As Psalm 46:10 reminds us, *"Be still, and know that I am God."* Jesus echoes this in Matthew 11:28–29, inviting us to come to *Him* and find rest for our souls.

When we are present with the Lord, we posture ourselves with open hands. We listen instead of rushing. We wait instead of forcing outcomes. We remain aware that the greatest gifts are not always visible, and the deepest blessings are often formed in quiet communion with Him.

In the kingdom of God, fruitfulness flows from receiving, not achieving. The world measures worth by production; God measures it by relationship. As Christ gives, we draw from His life, walk in His provision, and bears a yield that will last. This is the posture that transforms our striving into abiding, and our self-effort into Spirit-empowered living.

Shift from self-driven efforts of accomplishing results for Christ to receiving what He provides and seeing ourselves as He sees us.

Application: Five Ways of Receiving what will change us.

Receive all the Lord provides: eternal life, forgiveness, peace, spiritual power. We are filled with Christ, overflowing into others.

Receive with open hands and thankful hearts: humility that acknowledges everything is gift, not success (Ephesians 2:8–9).

Know your gifts and God's promises: identity in Christ breeds humility and dependence.

Steward what you have giving: plan and act faithfully (Matthew. 25:29). Give it away; it multiplies (1 Peter 4:10).

Renew your mind with eternal perspective: temporary results fade; only Spirit-empowered work lasts.

Who am I in God's eyes?

A primary application is to know who and whose you are – embrace your new identity. We are constantly in danger of letting the world define us instead of God, because it is so easy to do. It is only natural to shape our self-image by the attitudes and opinions of our parents, our peer groups, and our society. None of us are immune to the distorting effects of performance-based acceptance, and we can falsely conclude that we are worthless or that we must try to earn God's acceptance. It is only when we define ourselves by the truths of the Word rather than the thinking and experiences of the world that we can discover our deepest self.

When God says we are adopted into His family, that means we have gained a new perspective, a new heritage and a new future. Examine the list below. Reflect on who God says you are.

Who I am in Christ

I am accepted...

John 1:12	I am God's child.
John 15:15	As a disciple, I am a friend of Jesus Christ.
Romans 5:1	I have been justified.
1 Corinthians 6:17	I am united with the Lord, and I am one with Him in spirit.
1 Corinthians 6:19-20	I have been bought with a price and I belong to God.
1 Corinthians 12:27	I am a member of Christ's body.
Ephesians 1:3-8	I have been chosen by God and adopted as His child.
Colossians 1:13-14	I have been redeemed and forgiven of all my sins.

Colossians 2:9-10	I am complete in Christ.
Hebrews 4:14-16	I have direct access to the throne of grace through Jesus Christ.

I am secure…

Romans 8:1-2	I am free from condemnation.
Romans 8:28	I am assured that God works for my good in all circumstances.
Romans 8:31-39	I am free from any condemnation brought against me and I cannot be separated from the love of God.
2 Corinthians 1:21-22	I have been established, anointed and sealed by God.
Colossians 3:1-4	I am hidden with Christ in God.
Philippians 1:6	I am confident that God will complete the good work He started in me.
Philippians 3:20	I am a citizen of heaven.

I am significant…

John 15:5	I am a branch of Jesus Christ, the true vine, and a channel of His life.
John 15:16	I have been chosen and appointed to bear a harvest.
1 Corinthians 3:16	I am God's temple.
2 Corinthians 5:17-21	I am a minister of reconciliation for God.
Ephesians 2:6	I am seated with Jesus Christ in the heavenly realm.
Ephesians 2:10	I am God's workmanship.
Ephesians 3:12	I may approach God with freedom and confidence.
Philippians 4:13	I can do all things through Christ, Who strengthens me.

A person's identity must be defined, not by success or even significance, but solely based on Christ's sacrifice and His adoption of us into His family.

SHIFT #3   ACHIEVE TO RECEIVE   WHAT?

Our culture tells us that our worth is determined by our accomplishments and encourages us to pursue significance and meaning through the things we do. Scripture tells us that our worth is determined by what Christ was willing to do for us, and that in Him we have an unlimited and unchanging source of meaning and purpose. Who we are in Christ is not shaped by what we do, but by what He did on the cross and continues to do in our lives. It is not performance that determines our who we are; instead, our new position in Jesus becomes the basis for what we do. If we perceive ourselves to be worthless or inadequate this will be manifested in our behavior.

We honor God when we allow him to define us and tell us who we are regardless of our feelings or experiences to the contrary. In Christ, we are overcomers who have been adopted into God's family; set free from the bondage to Satan, sin, and death; called and equipped to accomplish an eternal purpose that will have enduring results; raised up with Christ and partakers of His life. Ken Boa

How do I live this way?

My worth and significance are found solely in Christ (which is forever and unchanging) and not in performance or in a position.

Because of my worth in Christ, I am free from the opinions of others, though I can listen and learn from them.

In this freedom from opinions, I can truly serve and love others (value and honor people).

Because of my security in Christ, I can be process-focused vs. results-oriented or bottom-line-driven.

Because of this freedom I possess, I can give away power or empower others, boldly and confidently.

"In Christ" I am free from the bondage to sin. That means I am free from one of the chief sins: pride. I need not "think more highly of myself than I ought."

His love and acceptance give me a security which helps me examine and purify my motives.

Andrew Murray: A Life of Abandonment and Power in Christ

Struggles of a Young Minister

Murray's early ministry was marked by self-reliance and an intense drive for success. He worked tirelessly, preached powerfully, and sought revival. However, he often operated in his own strength, not yet fully grasping the secret of abiding in Christ. This led to spiritual dryness and moments of discouragement.

A defining moment in his life came when he lost his voice due to overwork and a severe throat infection. For two years, he struggled to preach, and even after regaining some strength, his voice was permanently weakened. This period of silence forced him into deeper prayer and reflection, exposing his reliance on human effort rather than divine strength.

During the revival of 1860, Murray experienced a movement of the Holy Spirit that transformed his congregation. However, he initially struggled with the manifestations of emotion and enthusiasm, which challenged his theological framework. He had to learn humility and giving up as he realized that the work of the Spirit was beyond human control.

Discovering Christ as His Life and Peace

Murray's spiritual growth did not come overnight. Through trials, suffering, and deep reflection, he discovered the centrality of Christ as his life, peace, and power. The turning point was his absolute surrender. One of the most profound truths Murray learned was dying to self—the idea that the Christian life is not about trying harder but about yielding completely to Christ. This realization came through reading Scripture and personal suffering. His famous book, *Absolute Surrender*, captures this truth: *"God is ready to assume full responsibility for the life wholly yielded to Him."*

The Secret of Abiding in Christ.

The doctrine that changed Murray's life was John 15: Abiding in Christ. He came to see that Christ was not only his Savior but his very life. This led him to write one of his most influential works, *Abide in Christ*, where he emphasizes that the Christian life is lived not by self-effort, but by continual dependence on Christ. He wrote: *"Abiding in Christ is not a work that you have to do as a condition for enjoying His salvation, but a consenting to let Him do all for you, in you, and through you."*

Christ as Peace and Victory.

Murray learned that peace is not found in circumstances but in a yielded life hidden in Christ. He moved from striving to resting, from self-reliance to total dependence on the indwelling Christ. *"Do not strive in your own strength; cast yourself at the feet of the Lord Jesus and wait upon Him in the sure confidence that He is with you and works in you."* (Humility and Absolute Surrender)

Conclusion

Living as a Christian means learning to appropriate Christ—not just receiving salvation once, but receiving His ongoing grace, strength, and love daily. By focusing on receiving rather than achieving, we can rest in the sufficiency of Christ's work and grow in the deep, relational love that God desires with us. This shift in mindset transforms our spiritual life from a burdensome striving to a joyous, grace-filled journey with Christ.

Shift #3 Summary: Achieve → Receive (WHAT)

- From striving to resting in God's provision.
- Application: gratitude, stewardship, generosity.

Core Idea: The Christian life begins with receiving God's grace, then giving it away.

Practical Steps
1. Start with Gratitude – Write down three things you received from God today (life, forgiveness, opportunities).
2. Receive Before You Act – Pause before a task: acknowledge your dependence on His provision.

3. Give Generously – Share one resource (time, skill, money) as an act of receiving → giving.
4. Loosen Your Grip – Surrender one achievement you've tied your identity to.
5. Celebrate Grace, Not Performance – End your day naming where you saw God's provision, not your effort.

Reflection Questions
- Where do I measure my worth by achievements instead of grace?
- What blessings or provisions have I overlooked that I need to receive with gratitude?
- Do I give freely, or do I hold tightly to resources and recognition?
- How can I practice receiving from God before rushing to produce for Him?

SHIFT #3   ACHIEVE TO RECEIVE   WHAT?

Chapter Seven

Shift #4
King to Kingdom
HOW?

"If you read history, you will find that the Christians who did most for the present world were just those who thought most of the next. It is since Christians have largely ceased to think of the other world that they have become so ineffective in this. Aim at Heaven and you will get earth 'thrown in': aim at earth and you will get neither."
— C. S. Lewis

"But seek first the kingdom of God and his righteousness, and all these things will be added to you." **— Matthew 6:33**

Moving From King to Kingdom

This fourth shift—*from King to Kingdom*—is about moving from ruling our own little empires to living for the reign of Christ. It's about stepping down from the throne of self and taking our place as servants in the service of the Lord. It answers the *how* question of the Christian life: How will I live? How will I relate to others? How will I work, lead, and influence? It frames how we see people, our place in the world, and the calling we've been given.

Since the fall, the human heart has been bent toward self-rule—independence, self-protection, self-promotion, and control. This is true before Christ, and it can remain true even after we've trusted Him. Isaiah described it perfectly: *"We all, like sheep, have gone astray; each of us has turned to our own way" (Isaiah 53:6).* In our flesh, we like being in charge. We like calling the shots. We like being the "king" of our castle—and, if possible, the ruler over many.

But "being king" isn't about a title—it's a posture of the heart. It shows up when…

1. Final authority — want to be served, cling to control.
2. Manipulate people — use others as means to an end.
3. Crave applause — pride fuels performance.
4. Short-term focus — live for now, not the next life.
5. Idolize independence — "I don't need anyone."
6. Control outcomes — anger when things go wrong.
7. Success = privilege — measure worth by production.
8. Live for name/brand/comfort — reputation first.
9. Surround with "yes" people — avoid challenge.
10. Create fear culture — others only tell you what you want.
11. Thrive on command — telling people what/how to do.
12. Resist input — trust self over counsel.
13. Isolated and blind — no true friends, many blind spots.

Do you know anybody like this?

The truth is, we all have traces of this in us. Being "king" is simply when *self* is on the throne of your heart. You may follow Christ, but if this is your posture, you are still spiritually immature—often acting like a child in a crown.

Consider the Life Story of my close associate Wahid Wahba who truly models a "kingdom" heart. We have shared doing ministry in many countries in the Middle East and many times in Egypt. He is a modern-day apostle.

Wahid Wahba: From Religious Activity to Revolutionary Discipleship

I was born into a Christian home in Cairo, Egypt—a place where Christianity is often more about ministry than intimacy. On our government-issued ID cards, religion is not a private conviction but a public label. Growing up, being a Christian meant observing traditions, honoring family customs, and attending church on occasion. But a living, breathing relationship with Jesus? That was foreign to me.

All of that began to change when I was just 11 years old. I had a teacher in class who was the first genuine, born-again Christian I had ever met. His life radiated something different. He encouraged us to ask our parents for a Bible or even just a New Testament and to read one paragraph a day. That simple challenge sparked a lifelong seeking the Lord.

I started reading the Bible—day after day, paragraph by paragraph. And it wasn't long before I was completely drawn in. Jesus captivated me. His wisdom, His forgiveness, His compassion—I was in awe. Without anyone using the language of "conversion" or "born again," something real was happening inside of me. The Holy Spirit was already at work.

Within six months, the quiet change in my life became evident to my family. My father noticed. Then my mother. Soon, they too began to encounter Jesus for themselves. God wasn't just changing me—He was redeeming our entire family. In those early days, I became fascinated with the lives of missionaries. I wanted to give my life to God's work. But I also felt the need to study and prepare. I pursued dentistry and graduated from Cairo University in 1979. Yet even while I worked as a dentist for 15 years, ministry was never far from my heart.

I remember my first mission trip to Sudan, a moment that would mark the beginning of a new chapter. I had the privilege of presenting a Bible to the president of Sudan—a staunch Muslim leader. To my surprise, he kissed the Bible and placed it on his head as a sign of respect. That moment aired on public television and was printed in the newspapers the next day. It was a turning point for the Christian community in Sudan. They were emboldened. Encouraged. Their faith felt visible and validated.

SHIFT #4 KING TO KINGDOM HOW?

In 1994, I took a step of obedience and left dentistry to enter full-time ministry. God gave me a vision: to spread His Word throughout Egypt with spiritual depth and unity across denominations. I spent five years serving with the Egyptian Bible Society, traveling across the country, speaking in churches of every tradition, and witnessing God's Spirit move.

Then came a season of theological training and ministry across the Middle East. I joined Walk Thru the Bible, where I served for 17 years—12 of those in Egypt and five in the U.S., expanding the ministry internationally. But in 2018, God called me to another step of faith. I resigned and launched what would become my life's next calling: 4G3.

4G3 was born out of a deep burden—to serve the persecuted and displaced Church across the Middle East and beyond. We began as an extension of MELTI (Middle East Leadership Training Institute), which had been equipping believers since 2000. But 4G3 carried a new urgency, especially in light of the growing refugee crisis. We wanted to go deeper, wider, and farther into places where hope was scarce, and faith was costly. These Discipleship Institutes aren't tucked inside clean buildings; they're held in tents, under trees, in war-ravaged neighborhoods, and along refugee borders. We go where the Church is bleeding. And we help her heal.

Today, we have 4G3 Discipleship Institutes in places like Syria, Iraq, Sudan, Jordan, Lebanon, Egypt, Turkey, Pakistan, Ukraine, and across the African continent. By God's grace, we've reached over a million people. And we are only getting started.

This journey hasn't been without loss. In May 2024, my wife Laila and I sold our home in Egypt—a home that held decades of memories and represented our earthly inheritance. But through betrayal and deception, part of it was stolen by a family member. It was painful. And yet, when we read Hebrews 10, where believers "joyfully accepted the confiscation of their property because they knew they had better and lasting possessions," our hearts resonated deeply.

That passage reminded us of Colossians 3: "Since you have died, your life is hidden with Christ in God." We've come to see more clearly than ever: the eternal is our true home. What we left behind—our careers, our homeland, our comforts—is nothing compared to the surpassing worth of knowing Christ.

We do not feel we have sacrificed. How could we, when compared to the cross? Everything we have come to the end of self it has been a joy to lay down. Jesus gave everything for us. Our lives are simply a response to that kind of love. And so, we continue—one soul at a time, one institute at a time, one act of obedience at a time. For the persecuted Church. For the flourishing of faith under fire. For the glory of God. This is not just our ministry. This is our worship.

The King Complex: The Root of Control

At the root, the "king" mentality is about control, independence, and recognition. It's the inner pull to be at the center—of attention, decision-making, and success. And it's entirely possible to cover this with religious language or leadership jargon while still quietly building our own empire. When we operate as "ruler," our plans, our preferences, and our image become the focus.

Here are five ways "being the king" shows up—and how the Kingdom calls us to something better:

Self at the Center
> *Man:* Must have the final say, control the outcome, and be seen as indispensable.
> *Spiritual:* Christ calls us to crucify the self, not exalt it (Galatians 2:20).

Image Over Integrity
> *Man:* Obsessed with how things look—metrics, recognition, and optics.
> *Spiritual:* Jesus calls us to authenticity and humility, not perfectionism (Matthew 5:3).

Resistance to Correction
> *Man:* Surrounds themselves with "yes" people and avoids accountability.
> *Spiritual:* God calls us to humility and teachability (Proverbs 9:8–9; James 4:6).

Using People Instead of Serving Them
Man: Sees people as tools for a personal agenda.
Spiritual: In the Kingdom, leaders serve, not exploit (Mark 10:43–45).

Glory Seeking
Man: Wants credit, recognition, and applause.
Spiritual: "Not to us, O Lord, not to us, but to Your name be the glory" (Psalm 115:1).

The shift from King to Kingdom is radical because it requires complete abandonment—not just of what we do, but of who sits on the throne of our lives. It means living for the reign of Christ, where power is replaced by service, control by trust, and self-glory by God's glory. And in that exchange, we find the freedom, joy, and purpose we were made for.

The Gospel's Cure for the Ruler Mentality

The beautiful (and painful) truth is this: we all have a little "boss" inside of us. It shows up when we want to be in control, avoid consequences, or live as though we're the final authority. But Jesus doesn't shame us—He invites us to die to that false self and live in the freedom of the true self that is hidden with Christ in God (Colossians 3:3).

The cross is the cure. Not self-improvement, not behavior modification, but self-denial and resurrection life. As we give up our throne, we discover the peace, freedom, and fruitfulness that come from letting Christ rule.

What are the Dangers of "Being the King"

Isaiah 53:6 – "Each has turned to his own way"
1 Samuel 15 – Saul's partial obedience = rebellion
Luke 12:16-21 – The rich fool built his own empire

We are at enmity with the Lord. We are frustrated and angry at heart. You rely on yourself more than other and in fact you turn people away. One becomes isolated and alone which is an open door for the enemy to walk through. This attitude is full of pride, and the heart is insecure. The audience you want to please is self and you think the world is pleased also.

The ministry and church world are especially prone to this because it is so easy to take God's word and use it / manipulate it to get people to do what we want. We hide behind the cloak of religious activity and bible verses all the while it is self that is on the throne.

The consequences include: Isolation (people work *for* you, not *with* you). Burnout (you carry everything). Fear and frustration when things don't go your way. Pride, which blinds you to feedback or correction.

From King to Kingdom: Living the Shift Jesus Modeled

Jesus never operated from a throne of worldly power, yet He ruled with the authority of Heaven. In Mark 10:45, He offered a radical redefinition of leadership: *"The Son of Man did not come to be served, but to serve, and to give His life as a ransom for many."* In His time, to be a servant was to occupy the lowest position in society—someone with no rights, no recognition, and no worth outside of the one who owned them. Yet Jesus chose that very posture to model the heart of God's Kingdom. This was shocking then. It remains countercultural now—especially for those in positions of influence, leadership, or authority within the church or ministry. The way of Jesus is not the way of the crown, but the cross.

When we serve in God's Purposes, our posture changes. We stop treating our roles as positions to protect and start seeing them as assignments to fulfill. We don't use people to advance our plans—we serve them as image-bearers of God. We lead with humility, letting go of the illusion of control, and trusting God with the outcomes. Faithfulness becomes the measure of success, not performance. Maturity and obedience replace visibility and applause.

This shift shows up in practical ways. Instead of asking, "How do I win?" we begin to ask, "God, what do You want?" We listen more than we speak. We relinquish the need to control every detail or dominate every meeting. We stop comparing ourselves to others and start celebrating them. Our confidence no longer comes from results but from the One who called us. We are finally freed from the exhausting pressure of outcomes—because we know the results are God's responsibility, not ours.

At its core, Godly leadership is about trust. We move from controlling our lives to trusting the One who gave us life. We shift from ownership to stewardship—recognizing that everything we have is on loan from God. Our dreams and plans no longer revolve around building our own empire but advancing His purposes.

The signs of whether we're still sitting on the throne—or allowing Christ to reign—are often subtle but revealing. When we resist feedback, fear losing control, or measure our worth by success and image, we're still functioning like the lead dog. When we strive for recognition or cling tightly to our plans, we're building our own empire, not His. But when we daily seek God's will, steward people and resources with care, repent quickly, and freely celebrate the success of others, we are living as servants. These are the marks of someone who has stepped off the throne and into God's way.

And the results of this shift are nothing short of transformational. You begin to experience freedom, because you're no longer burdened with outcomes that were never yours to carry. You gain purpose, because your work now has eternal value beyond the moment. You find peace, because your soul rests under the rule of a trustworthy leader. And you demonstrate Christ—not just through your gifts or strength, but through the Spirit of God working in and through your surrendered life. Your leadership begins to bless others and honor God. This is not just better leadership. It's a better life.

Our Work in God's Kingdom

As followers of Christ, we are all called to work, the key is the motive or reason behind our work that is important to the Lord and what makes any endeavor eternally fruitful or not. All work that is done either from the most menial task or a world changing ministry is equal in God's eyes, if done with a spiritual heart and motive. Too often, we focus on the type of work we do and make a value judgment that ministry is more spiritual than work done in the marketplace or the home. Nothing could be further from the truth. The principle is this: secular work done with a spiritual heart is spiritually fruitful in God's eyes and spiritual work done with a secular heart is totally unfruitful in God's eyes. So, when we work with a heart of serving God and putting others first it produces true eternal impact and fruit.

Application

Questions: Reflect and Respond
Where in my life am I still "sitting on the throne"?
What does dying to self-look like practically this week?
How can I use my leadership or influence to serve others?

The following are four ways we can make application of this shift. This is reflected in the verse in second Timothy where we are called to be strengthened by God's grace and yet then be able to serve and teach other people. "Quit trying to be in charge, having people to meet our needs or tell people what to do." 2 Timothy 2:1–2, *"You then, my child, be strengthened by the grace that is in Christ Jesus… entrust to faithful men who will be able to teach others also."*

Specific Application
A Servant Heart — Release the role of ruler, embrace Christ's reign. Have spiritual motive of serving Christ as you serve others.
God's Will Only — Prioritize obedience, not outcomes. Put your will and desires in neutral.
An Eternal Perspective — Live with heaven in view. How we view life drives how we do life.
A Ministry Lifestyle — See all of our work as ministry if done with the right heart.

Doing God's Will is Key to Kingdom Living

If we are in God's will we are in the best and only place that God wants us. The following is a process used by George Mueller to find and walk in God's will. Here is how he summed up the way he entered into a "heart" relationship with God and learned to discern God's voice:

1. *I seek at the beginning to get my heart into such a state that it has no will of its own in regard to a given matter. Nine-tenths of the trouble with people generally is just here. Nine-tenths of the difficulties are overcome when*

our hearts are ready to do the knowledge of what His will is. We must be neutral to hear God's will.

2. *Having done this, I do not leave the result to feeling or simple impression. If so, I make myself liable to great delusions.*
3. *I seek the Will of the Spirit of God through, or in connection with, the Word of God. The Spirit and the Word must be combined. If I look to the Spirit alone without the Word, I lay myself open to great delusions also. If the Holy Ghost guides us at all, He will do it according to the Scriptures and never contrary to them.*
4. *Next, I take into account providential circumstances. These often plainly indicate God's will in connection with His Word and Spirit.*
5. *I ask God in prayer to reveal His Will to me aright.*
6. *Thus, (1) through prayer to God, (2) The study of the Word, and (3) reflection, I come to a deliberate judgment according to the best of my ability and knowledge, and if my mind is thus at peace, and continues so after two or three more petitions, I proceed.*

Summary   **Die daily:** Die to the need to rule or be seen.
Depend deeply: Draw strength from grace, not gifting.
Labor faithfully: Serve where you are, multiply disciples, glorify Christ.

Concept	What It Is	What It's Not	What It Means...
Kingdom Living	Surrendering your life to Christ's reign; seeking His kingdom first (Matthew 6:33).	Ruling your own life, building your own platform or success.	Letting go of control, living under His authority, serving others.
Servant Heart	Prioritizing others above yourself; following Jesus' example (Mark 10:45).	Seeking position, title, or recognition; prideful self-reliance.	Humbly serving, letting go of rights and entitlements, embracing hidden faithfulness.
Eternal Perspective	Living with heaven in view; focusing on what lasts eternally (Colossians 3:1–2).	Prioritizing temporary gains, influence, and comfort.	Investing in the eternal, giving up what you can't keep to gain what you can't lose.
Ministry Lifestyle	A generational, disciple-making calling (2 Timothy 2:1–2); everyone's role in ministry.	Ministry as a career, platform, or personal identity.	Engaging fully in making disciples wherever you are; being all-in for the kingdom.

Illustration: The Servant Life of Oswald Chambers

Before he became the beloved voice behind *My Utmost for His Highest*, Chambers was a man of remarkable talent. Born in Scotland in 1874, he displayed artistic brilliance, spiritual sensitivity, and academic sharpness from an early age. He was passionate about truth, deeply committed to Christ, and widely admired by peers for his insight and intensity. During his time at Dunoon College, he seemed a rising star in the Christian world. Yet beneath the outward strength was a restless heart. He longed not only to serve Christ but to experience His power and presence in a way that went beyond sermons and study.

Chambers, like so many earnest believers, was full of effort—but empty of peace. His life, though gifted and zealous, still bore the marks of someone trying to do for Jesus more than someone who allows Christ to live through him.

The Breaking Point: Death to Self, Life in the Spirit

That inner conflict came to a head in his early twenties. Despite being active in ministry, Chambers reached a spiritual breaking point. His prayers felt dry, his efforts hollow. He knew the language of faith but lacked the power. And so, in a season of wrestling, he reached what he would later call his "white funeral"—the moment he died to self.

"I was at my wit's end," he would later recall. "Then I saw it—I had been asking God for power on my own terms. I gave up. I said, 'Lord, I don't care if You never bless me again. I belong to You.'" That simple, agonizing surrender marked the end of Chambers' reign—and the beginning of the God's rule in his life. It wasn't an emotional high or instant breakthrough. But it was the beginning of supernatural growth. Christ now ruled from within.

Christ in and Through Him

From that point on, Chambers' life took on a new tone. He was no less passionate, but now there was peace. He was no less active, but now it was Christ working through him. Those who heard him teach noted not just insight, but spiritual authority—something that couldn't be learned, only imparted. His wife Biddy, who later compiled and published his teachings, observed that people were drawn not to Oswald, but to the presence of Christ within him.

Chambers' message changed too. He no longer emphasized trying hard for God but instead being fully yielded to Him. "The destined end of man," he wrote, "is not happiness, nor health, but holiness." He no longer sought results but a love with Christ. No longer outcomes but appropriating. He had moved from self-led service to a Spirit-empowered life.

A Quiet Legacy

In 1917, Chambers died unexpectedly of complications from appendicitis at the age of 43. He never knew how far-reaching his influence would become. He had no bestseller during his lifetime, no global platform. Yet today, *My Utmost for His Highest* remains one of the most widely read Christian devotionals in history.

Finally, we begin to measure success not by visible results, but by invisible faithfulness. Oswald Chambers didn't see the product of his faithfulness in his lifetime—and that's the point. Last difference often happens long after we stop trying to make it happen.

Christ Within You

Oswald Chambers once wrote, *"God is not preparing us for a place, but for Himself."* That's the heart of the transformed life. It's not about becoming a spiritual giant. It's not about producing perfect outcomes. It's about yielding so fully to Christ that His life flows through ours. It's about stepping off the throne, handing Him the crown, and saying: "Your Kingdom come. Your will be done—in me, and through me."

Shift #4 Summary: King → Kingdom (WHERE)

- Serving the Kingdom, not building personal empires.
- Application: humility, people-focused vision.

Core Idea: Life is not about building your own kingdom but serving Christ's Kingdom.

Practical Steps
1. Reframe Goals – Rewrite one personal ambition in Kingdom terms (e.g., career → "impact coworkers for Christ").
2. Serve First – Choose one unnoticed act of service each day. your dependence on His provision.
3. Evaluate Audience – Ask: "Am I doing this for my glory, or God's?"
4. People Over Projects – Intentionally value relationships above results.
5. Pray Kingdom Prayers – Regularly pray Matthew 6:10: "Your Kingdom come, Your will be done."

Reflection Questions
- Where am I still building my own kingdom instead of serving His?
- Who around me have I treated as "projects" rather than people of eternal value?
- What personal goals need to be reframed in light of God's Kingdom?
- How can I practice humility and service in a specific relationship this week?

SHIFT #4   KING TO KINGDOM   HOW?

Chapter Eight

Shift #5
Trials to Triumph
WHICH?

"The will of God is never exactly what you expect it to be. It may seem much worse, but in the end, it's going to be a lot better and a lot bigger." — **Elisabeth Elliot**

"In all this you greatly rejoice, though now for a little while you may have had to suffer grief in all kinds of trials. These have come so that the proven genuineness of your faith—of greater worth than gold…may result in praise, glory and honor when Jesus Christ is revealed." — **1 Peter 1:6–7**

Observations about Trials

Pain and difficulties are real and sometimes longer term.
Life is lived in the valley, not on the mountaintop.
God will use problems to grow us in ways we could not, especially our faith.
God is using the challenges to prepare us for future opportunities.
How we handle the difficulties reveals our maturity and will shape us.
We are to be thankful and hopeful in the struggle – know that we are not alone.

Victory is obtained in the journey, not in the outcome. It is based in Christ – His purposes and our mindset.

From Trials to Triumph

Many believers settle for mere survival—enduring hardship with quiet resignation or loud bitterness, feeling powerless against the weight of their trials. Life becomes a constant holding pattern, waiting for circumstances to improve or for the storm to pass. But Christ calls us to more. He calls us to rise above circumstances and live victoriously in Him. He never promised an easy life, but He promised His presence in the storm and His ultimate triumph over every enemy we face.

Trials are real, but they do not define us. Pain is present, but Christ's presence is greater. The enemy is active, but he is already defeated. The struggle is real, but His triumph is certain. This is not wishful thinking—it is the unshakable reality of life in Christ.

The Christian life in this fallen world is difficult because we live in a battleground, not a playground. Sin is everywhere, Satan is relentless, and our own flesh wars against the Spirit within us. We face trials that touch every part of life: health crises, relational conflicts, financial pressures, opposition for our faith, spiritual dryness, persecution, temptation, and loss. These are not minor inconveniences; they are the grinding realities of living in a world that groans for redemption.

Yet the gospel reframes every battle. Winning in the fight of life is not about avoiding hardship—it is about transforming hardship into holy ground. It is about letting trials become the tools God uses to shape us into the likeness of Christ, deepen our faith, and multiply the difference we make. As James wrote, the testing of our faith produces perseverance, and perseverance, when it finishes its work, makes us *"mature and complete, not lacking anything" (James 1:4).*

This shift—from being defeated by fear, circumstances, or the enemy, to walking in the triumph we already have in Christ—is critical. It is the difference between living as a victim of life's blows and living as *"more than a conqueror through Him who loved us" (Romans 8:37).* It requires a decisive choice: to stop complaining and struggling in our own strength and instead trust the Lord to work through the trial, to lead us into His conquest, and to turn our testing into a testimony.

The way forward is not pretending pain isn't real or denying the hardship. It is learning to see the battle through the eyes of faith. It is knowing that no trial is wasted, no wound is unseen, and no enemy is stronger than our Savior. When we choose to trust Him fully in the fire, we discover the power of His promise: that He works all things—even the hardest things—for our good and His glory.

This chapter will show how to make that shift. How to fight with the weapons God provides. How to anchor your heart in the hope of His Word. And how to let the trials you face today become the triumphs of forever.

Many believers settle for just surviving—enduring hardship with resignation or bitterness, feeling powerless against trials. But Christ calls us to more: to rise above circumstances and live victoriously in Him. He never promised an easy life, but He promised His presence.

Shifting from being defeated by fear, circumstance or the enemy and step in the victory we have in Christ.

"Quit complaining and struggling. Trust the Lord to work and walk you into His conquest.

Triumph Through Christ

Overcoming in the Christian life does not come from avoiding hardship—it comes from walking through hardship with Christ. The battles you face are real, but so is the victory He has already secured. Scripture gives us a clear pathway to live in that victory, not just in theory, but in daily practice.

There are four essential steps to application:
1. **Peace in the Pain – Trusting His Presence in Every Circumstance**
   The starting point is peace—peace that comes not from the absence of trouble, but from the presence of Christ. Life's pain is unavoidable, but you are never alone in it. Jesus promised, *"In this world you*

will have trouble. But take heart! I have overcome the world" (John 16:33). His triumph is not future—it is present.

Philippians 4:6-7 gives us the pattern: refuse anxiety, present every request to God, and appropriate His peace that surpasses understanding. This is more than a comforting feeling—it's the supernatural guard for your heart and mind.

When you anchor yourself in His presence, trials lose their power to control you. As James 1:2-4 reminds us, trials are not dead ends; they are tools in God's hands to grow perseverance, maturity, and completeness. Peace in pain is an act of trust—it declares that God's plan is bigger than the storm.

2. **Position – Seated with Christ, Secure and Victorious**
Security is not something you work toward—it's a position you've already been given. Ephesians 2:6 declares that God has raised us up and seated us with Christ in the heavenly realms. This is not wishful thinking; it's a spiritual reality.

Your position in Christ means you fight from victory, not for victory. Colossians 3:1 urges us to set our hearts on things above, where Christ is. Keeping an eternal view reframes your temporary struggles. Romans 8:28 assures us that in *all things*, God is working for the good of those who love Him—your position guarantees that even what the enemy means for harm, God can turn into good.

When you know where you are seated, you no longer live as a victim of circumstance. You live as one who is secure, chosen, and already part of Christ's unshakable kingdom.

3. **Practice – Walk Worthy of Your Calling**
The practice is not passive—it is lived out daily. It is two-fold: walking worthy and not walking alond. Ephesians 4:1 calls us to *walk in a manner worthy of the calling.* Colossians 1:10 expands it: *"Live a life worthy of the Lord and please Him in every way: bearing fruit in every good work, growing in the knowledge of God."*

Walking worthy means refusing to shrink back in difficulty. It means choosing obedience even when it costs. It means using your trial as a platform for ministry—serving others who are hurting, speaking hope into dark places, and demonstrating the reality of Christ through your perseverance. As 2 Corinthians 12:9–10 teaches, your weakness is not a liability—it is the stage for God's power to be displayed. Walking worthy is leaning on His strength, not your own, and letting your steps reflect His character.

Walk with others in the valleys. When we are vulnerable and willing to serve others we build relationships. These are what sustain us and support us. In the challenges. Ecclesiastes 4:9-12 tells us the two are better than one. Lean into others as you walk through the difficulties.

4. **Protection – Stand Firm in the Armor of God**
Standing firm also requires vigilance. You have a real enemy whose mission is to steal, kill, and destroy. Ephesians 6:13 tells us to take up the full armor of God so we can stand firm in the evil day. Standing firm is not about aggression—it's about immovability, refusing to be pushed back from the ground Christ has won for you.

James 4:7 gives the two-fold strategy: *submit to God* and *resist the devil*. Submission keeps you under God's authority; resistance keeps you engaged in the fight. 1 Peter 1:6–7 reminds us that even in suffering, our faith is being refined like gold, resulting in praise, glory, and honor when Christ is revealed.

Standing firm means knowing your weapons—truth, righteousness, the gospel of peace, faith, salvation, and the Word of God—and using them daily. It means praying without ceasing, guarding your heart, and refusing the enemy's lies.

Trials will come—but triumph is your inheritance in Christ. When you live with peace in the pain, stand in your position, practice your calling, and put on God's protection, you experience what John 16:33 promises: trouble in the world, yes, but unshakable victory in Him. WHICH of these will be your focus? These principles apply before adversity hits, while you're in the middle of it, or when you're helping others through it.

1. **See the good in the bad.** Be the person who can find the bright side in a difficult situation and keep challenges in perspective. This isn't about being unrealistic or naive, it's about looking adversity in the eye and focusing on what you can control.
2. **Help others as you go.** Serve others – it helps you focus and show you that you are not alone. Stay connected, navigate the storm together, and remember: calm is contagious.
3. **It doesn't get easier, you get stronger.** Struggle triggers growth. Failure is feedback. Losing teaches. Setbacks set up comebacks.
4. **Let pain become fuel.** Don't let difficulty blind you to the opportunity inside it. The struggle you're in now could be the very thing that shapes your best self later.
5. **Remember: it's part of the process.** You will question why you started, and that's normal. Obstacles test how badly you want it. See them as stepping stones to where you want to go.

Adversity will not wait for you to be ready. Decide now how you'll respond as the leader because the next challenge could be the one that will define you and your team.

Victory is Ours and It is Sure In Christ

Simply reflect and remind yourself of that Christ has already won the victory.

Psalms 23:4-6, *"Even though I walk through the valley of the shadow of death, I fear no evil, for You are with me; Your rod and Your staff, they comfort me. You prepare a table before me in the presence of my enemies; You have anointed my head with oil; My cup overflows.*

Surely goodness and lovingkindness will follow me all the days of my life, and I will dwell in the house of the Lord forever."

Romans 8:37, "No, despite all these things, overwhelming victory is ours through Christ, who loved us."

1 Corinthians 15:54-57, "But when this perishable will have put on the imperishable, and this mortal will have put on immortality, then will come about the saying that is written, "Death is swallowed up in victory. 55O death, where is your victory? O death, where is your sting?" 56The sting of death is sin, and the power of sin is the law; 57but thanks be to God, who gives us the victory through our Lord Jesus Christ. 58 Therefore, my beloved brethren, be steadfast, immovable, always abounding in the work of the Lord, knowing that your toil is not in vain in the Lord.

2 Corinthians 2:14, "thanks be to God who always leads us in **triumph** and manifests through us the sweet aroma of the knowledge of Him in every place. "

Philippians 4:11-13, "I have learned to be content in whatever circumstances I am. 12I know how to get along with humble means, and I also know how to live in prosperity; in any and every circumstance I have learned the secret of being filled and going hungry, both of having abundance and suffering need. 13I can do all things through Him who strengthens me."

1 John 5:4, "For whatever is born of God overcomes the world; and this is the **victory** that has overcome the world—our faith."

Key Application - Living the Paradoxes

The Christian life is filled with paradoxes—seemingly contradictory truths that, when understood and lived out, bring us into deeper communion with God. These paradoxes counter the world's wisdom and even challenge the way many Christians typically approach faith. These paradoxes challenge human wisdom and invite believers into a deeper, more transformative relationship with God, as they reflect on how His ways often contradict human expectations.

Many Christians, though sincere in their faith, often find themselves caught between the world's values and God's ways. We tend to equate strength with self-sufficiency, success with power, and freedom with autonomy. Even in the church, leadership can become about influence rather than service, and suffering is often seen as something to be avoided rather than embraced as a refining tool in God's hands. The paradoxes of the Christian life disrupt our natural inclinations:

We want control, but God calls us to give up.
We want comfort, but God calls us to embrace suffering for His sake.
We seek personal greatness, but God calls us to be servants.
We want quick results, but God works through long-term faithfulness.

To embrace these paradoxes is to reject self-centered faith and adopt a radical trust in God. The Christian life is often characterized by several paradoxes—seemingly contradictory statements or concepts that, when deeply understood, offer profound truths. Here are some key paradoxes of the Christian life:

Strength through Weakness: Christianity teaches that in our weakness; God's strength is most evident. This is reflected in the apostle Paul's writing, where he says, *"For when I am weak, then I am strong" (2 Corinthians 12:10)*. Christians believe that God often works through the weak and humble, not through the powerful or self-sufficient.

The Last Shall Be First: Jesus repeatedly taught that those who humble themselves will be exalted. The concept of *"the first shall be last and the last shall be first" (Matthew 20:16)* challenges the typical social structures and human understanding of power, success, and status.

Freedom Through Obedience: Christianity teaches that true freedom is found in submission to God's will. In a world that often associates freedom with self-rule, the Bible teaches that obeying God's commandments leads to freedom from sin and its consequences. Jesus says, *"If you hold to my teaching, you are really my disciples. Then you will know the truth, and the truth will set you free" (John 8:31-32).*

Growth Through Suffering: Many Christians face trials and sufferings, yet they are taught to find joy in them. *James 1:2-3 "Consider it pure joy, my brothers and sisters, whenever you face trials of many kinds, because you know that the testing of your faith produces perseverance."* The paradox is that suffering can lead to spiritual growth and blessings that are not be possible without it.

Lose your life to find it. *"For whoever wants to save their life will lose it, but whoever loses their life for me will find it" Matthew 16:25.* Jesus is saying that focusing solely on self-preservation and earthly gain will ultimately lead to a loss of true meaning and purpose, while prioritizing faith and following him will lead to a richer, eternal life.

It Will Cost Us

There is no way to live this kind of life without cost. Jesus Himself said, *"Whoever wants to be my disciple must deny themselves and take up their cross daily and follow me" (Luke 9:23).* Here's what embracing these paradoxes will cost:

Our pride (we must admit our weakness).
Our desire for control (we must yield to God's ways).
Our pursuit of personal gain (we must live for God and others).
Our comfort (we must endure trials and hardships).
Our reputation (we may be misunderstood or even rejected for living differently).

The cost is real, but so is the reward. Jesus promises that those who lose their lives for His sake will find true life.

A Life of Faith - Hudson Taylor

Hudson Taylor, a pioneering British missionary to China, faced significant struggles before discovering the deeper meaning of living the

"Christ life." Initially, Taylor struggled with a sense of personal inadequacy and spiritual dryness. Though he was deeply committed to his mission, he often felt frustrated by his inability to live up to his own standards of faith. He experienced a period of deep spiritual crisis, feeling that despite his best efforts, he wasn't living the victorious Christian life he longed for.

One of the key struggles Taylor faced was his reliance on his own efforts and self-discipline in his work and spiritual life, rather than trusting fully in God's grace and strength. He felt disconnected from the power of God in his personal life and missionary work. This led to exhaustion and a sense of defeat, as his reliance on self was unfruitful.

The turning point came when Taylor read a pamphlet by an evangelist named William C. Burns that emphasized the idea of living in full dependence on God's grace and strength. He realized that the Christian life was not about striving in his own strength but about living in the reality of Christ's life within him. This realization led to a profound shift in his spiritual life, and Taylor began to experience a deeper sense of peace, joy, and power in his walk with God. He came to understand that Christ himself, living through him, would empower him for ministry, allowing him to serve with greater effectiveness and joy. This discovery of the "Christ life" was foundational to his continued work and success as a missionary in China.

Final Call to Action: Challenge for all Believers

> "Will you rise up as a warrior-leader—not in your own strength, but fully armed in Christ, yielded, vigilant, and steadfast?"
> "The devil trembles when he sees the weakest saint on his knees."
> — William Cowper
> "Triumph is not about defeating Satan—it's about standing in the One who already has."— Ken Boa

You are not alone. You are not abandoned. You are not powerless. In Christ, the war is won. Now take your stand.

Shift #5 Summary: Trials → Triumph (WHICH)

- Embracing brokenness as part of God's plan. Being thankful in everything.
- Application: perseverance, gratitude, reliance on Christ.

Core Idea: Brokenness and suffering are tools God uses for growth and ministry.

Practical Steps
1. Reframe Struggles – Identify one trial and ask: "How can God use his for growth or ministry?"
2. Practice Gratitude in Pain – Write one thing you're thankful for even in difficulty.
3. Lean on Community – Share your struggle with a trusted believer instead of carrying it alone.
4. Anchor in Scripture – Memorize verses on endurance (e.g., James 1:2–4, Romans 8:28).
5. Encourage Someone Else – Use your trial to comfort or support another in need.

Reflection Questions
- What current trial am I resisting instead of submitting to God's shaping?
- Where can I choose gratitude today in the middle of difficulty?
- Who could I encourage by sharing how God is meeting me in my struggle?
- How have past trials grown my faith or given me opportunities to minister?

SHIFT #5   TRIALS TO TRIUMPH   WHICH?

Chapter Nine

Eternal Impact

"The things that are eternal are the most real things of all."
— A. W. Tozer

"So, we fix our eyes not on what is seen, but on what is unseen, since what is seen is temporary, but what is unseen is eternal."
— 2 Corinthians 4:18

Living for What Lasts: The Perspective of Eternal Impact

We live in a world obsessed with the temporary—chasing success, accumulating possessions, and curating moments that vanish as quickly as they come. But deep down, we all know the truth: not everything we pour our lives into will last.

The question that changes everything is this:

What truly lasts forever?

As we shift our perspective and live with an eternal mindset it will yield five things that will last forever.

Shift		Eternal Outcome
Chist-Like to Christ Life	→	An intimate relationship with Christ.
For Christ to From Christ	→	Much Fruit and living God's unchanging Word.

Achieving to Receiving	→	Eternal rewards we will be given in heaven.
King to Kingdom	→	The spirit and soul of people who come to Christ
Trial to Triumph	→	Your worship, praise, and thanksgiving that glorify God Himself.

When these five priorities take center stage in your heart, mind, and daily actions, your life gains an entirely new trajectory. You begin to live for the things that last. You glorify the Lord in ways that will bless you forever.

We Are Eternal Beings in a Temporary World

The danger is that we confuse the temporary for the eternal and end up living for what cannot last. But when we live with eternity in view, our impact becomes far-reaching—touching lives, shaping hearts, and storing up treasure where it will never fade.

The Reality of Eternal Impact

Heaven is a reality: the way you live today will echo forever in God's Kingdom. Every prayer whispered in faith, every act of quiet obedience, every word of truth spoken in love, every burden carried with grace—none of it is wasted.

James reminds us that our trials produce perseverance, which matures us for eternal purposes (James 1:2–4). Paul tells us that God works all things—even the hard and painful things—for our good and His glory (Romans 8:28). Peter declares that the testing of our faith refines it like gold, resulting in praise and honor when Christ is revealed (1 Peter 1:6–7).

When you live for what lasts, you stop asking, *"What can I gain now?"* and start asking, *"What will matter forever?"*

You invest in the things God values most, confident that heaven will reveal the full story of your life's impact.

Worth It All

One day, you will see Christ face to face. On that day, the allure of temporary accomplishments will fade, and the beauty of eternal investment will shine brighter than the sun. You will see how He used your life—your prayers, your sacrifices, your service—to touch others. And you will know, without a doubt, that living for what lasts was worth it all.

This is the invitation before you—not just to believe in the next life, but to live every day in light of it. The world will pull you toward the fleeting; Christ calls you toward the forever. The choice is yours.

D. L. Moody – From Self-Driven Labor to Spirit-Empowered Ministry

In the early years of his ministry, Dwight L. Moody was a man of relentless energy and tireless work ethic. He was deeply passionate about evangelism, conducting Sunday schools, and street preaching. By all outward appearances, he was doing everything right. He was busy for the Lord—but inwardly, he was still the king. He was the planner, the driver, the doer.

Despite his efforts, the evidence of his ministry was limited. Crowds came, but conversions were few. He grew frustrated. He sensed something vital was missing, though he couldn't put his finger on it. He was laboring in his own strength, and the results showed it.

Then something happened that changed everything.

Two elderly women often sat in the front row during his meetings in Chicago. He noticed them praying intensely throughout his messages. Eventually, they approached him and said, *"Mr. Moody, we're praying that you may get the power of the Holy Spirit."*

Moody was puzzled—even a bit offended. Wasn't he already serving God with all he had? But their words struck a chord. He began seeking God earnestly, asking for more of the Holy Spirit—for true power from above, not just human energy.

Then came a moment of deep brokenness.

While in New York City, Moody was walking the streets, burdened and desperate for a touch from God. In his own words, he said: "One day, in the city of New York—oh, what a day! —I cannot describe it; I seldom refer to it; it is almost too sacred an experience to name... I can only say that God revealed Himself to me, and I had such an experience of His love that I had to ask Him to stay His hand."

That day marked a turning point.

Moody returned to his ministry not with more energy, but with less of *him*. The same sermons, the same methods—but now filled with the power of the Holy Spirit. The results were staggering. Lives began to change. Conversions came by the hundreds, then thousands. It wasn't because Moody had become a better speaker. It was because he had moved from being the king of his ministry to being a vessel for the Kingdom.

He once said: *"The world has yet to see what God can do with a man fully consecrated to Him."*

Reflection

Just like D. L. Moody, many Christians can be busy doing things for God, yet never truly transformed by Him. The shift from self-driven leadership to Spirit-led living is the essence of Romans 12:2—no longer conformed to the world's values of control, outcomes, and self-importance, but transformed into servants of the King.

Everyday Ways to Live with Eternity in Mind

When we think of eternal living, our minds often leap to grand callings—missionaries who leave everything behind, leaders who shape history, or martyrs who lay down their lives. But the truth is, most of us won't be called to those stages. Instead, eternity is woven into the fabric of our ordinary, daily faithfulness. The small decisions we make each day, when surrendered to Christ, ripple into forever.

Parenting with Eternity in View

Raising children is one of the most sacred callings of stewardship. Every bedtime prayer, every Scripture verse memorized at the kitchen table, every conversation about God's truth sows seeds that outlast us. Parents live eternally-minded when they see themselves not just as caretakers but as disciple-makers, entrusted with shaping souls who belong first to the Lord.

Work as Worship

Most of life is lived not in pulpits or mission fields but in offices, classrooms, and workplaces. When we approach our work with integrity, excellence, and service, we declare that Christ is Lord over all. Work done unto Him—whether closing a deal, teaching a student, or repairing a roof—becomes eternal when it reflects His character and advances His kingdom through our witness.

Generosity that Outlives Us

Every act of generosity—whether financial, practical, or relational—is an investment in eternity. Writing a check to support gospel work, sharing a meal with a neighbor in need, or giving time to mentor someone younger in the faith are all ways to store up treasure in heaven. Generosity shifts our hearts from clinging to what will fade to holding fast to what will last.

Worship in the Everyday

Worship is more than a Sunday gathering—it is a posture of the heart. Singing in the car, thanking God while washing dishes, or pausing to pray in the middle of a busy day are simple but eternal acts. These moments tether our hearts to the eternal presence of God and remind us that life is not measured in minutes but in meaning.

Living for what lasts is not reserved for extraordinary moments—it is forged in the ordinary ones. When we parent, work, give, and worship with eternity in view, we join Abraham, who *"looked forward to the city with* *foundations, whose architect and builder is God" (Hebrews 11:10)*. Eternity is not just ahead of us; it is breaking into our lives right now, through the faithfulness of daily surrender.

Conclusion

Kingdom impact begins with Christ Himself being our source of life and power, then living in us as we fully rest in Him. From there, we take hold of His gifts and promises, using them and giving them away. Our focus shifts from control and self to the Kingdom of God and serving people. Even while living in a world of challenges and pain, we find blessing in the journey.

We then experience a forever difference by glorifying and worshiping God, growing in His Word, seeing people come to Christ and be discipled, and laying up treasure in heaven. For truly, *where our treasure is, there our heart will be also.*

Chapter Ten

Practical Impact Framework

"Do not work for food that spoils, but for food that endures to eternal life, which the Son of Man will give you." — **John 6:27**

Putting It All Together – A Personal Framework

In the preceding chapters, we discussed five spiritual shifts in perspective that lead to an abundant, lasting life both now and forever. To make this practical, here are five corresponding ways to live it out. Each piece fits into a life of impact:

Practical Impact Framework Summary: Living for What Lasts

Shift	Core Question	Key Truth	Practical Actions
1. Christlike → Christ Life (WHO)	Who is my source?	Not imitation, but Christ living in me.	CORE VALUES: Surrender daily, Appropriate His promises, Be Spirit-led in decisions, Replace effort with rest, Reflect & record
2. For Christ → From Christ (WHY)	Why am I doing this?	Ministry flows from intimacy with Christ.	PURPOSE: Abide first, Pray "through me" not "help me", Check motives, Guard relationships, Weekly reset
3. Achieve → Receive (WHAT)	What defines my actions?	Grace received, then given.	MISSION: Start with gratitude, Receive before acting, Give generously, Loosen your grip, Celebrate grace
4. King → Kingdom (WHERE)	Where is my focus?	Build God's Kingdom, not my own.	VISION: Reframe goals, Serve first, Evaluate audience, People over projects, Pray Kingdom prayers
5. Trials → Triumph (WHICH)	How do I face challenges?	God uses suffering for growth & ministry.	PROBLEM YOU SOLVE: Reframe struggles, Gratitude in pain, Lean on community, Anchor in Scripture, Encourage someone else

Let's take these five practical applications and build them out.

Element	Definition	Question It Answers	Function
Core Values *Christ as Life*	Anchors that guide your life in Christ	"What is most important to me because of who Christ is in me?"	Ground your decisions and behaviors
Purpose *From Christ*	Why God created you uniquely	"Why am I here?"	Provides direction and meaning
Mission *Receiving*	What you are called to do regularly	"What am I called to do today to fulfill my purpose?"	Drives daily action
Vision *Kingdom*	A Spirit-led picture of your future impact	"What does a life of eternal impact look like?"	Inspires perseverance and big-picture thinking
Problem You Solve *Triumph*	The need or pain you are uniquely equipped to address	"Whose lives am I meant to influence and how?"	Connects your purpose with others' growth

Living It Out – A Practical Process

Living for what lasts isn't just an inspiring idea—it's a daily way of life. To build a life that has lasting change, you need more than good intentions; you need clarity. The following process will help you define, align, and live out your God-given calling.

1. Clarify Your Core Values

Your core values are Christ-honoring convictions that define how you live and make decisions. They act as guardrails, ensuring your choices align with God's heart.

Why Core Values Count

They anchor you in Christ's character.
They keep you from drifting.
They clarify who you are becoming.
They shape your legacy.

Process:

List 3–5 values that reflect Christ's character (e.g., humility, generosity, courage, faithfulness).

Ask: Would these values make sense in heaven?

Notice repeated themes in Scripture that God keeps bringing to your attention.

Practical Step: Write a brief definition for each value and give a real-life example of how it looks in action.

1.
2.
3.
4.
5.

Core values are not a self-improvement tool—they are a discipleship tool. They help us remain in the Vine, express His life in tangible ways, and ensure that the impact we make is the result of Christ living through us, not us striving in our own strength.

2. Discover Your Purpose

Purpose is not just a statement—it's a Spirit-led conviction about why you exist. It's the unique way God designed you to glorify Him and serve others.

Reflection Questions:

What breaks my heart?

What brings me joy when done for God's glory?

What gifts, strengths, and life experiences (both joyful and painful) have God entrusted to me?

"For we are His workmanship, created in Christ Jesus for good works…"
— *Ephesians 2:10*

Clarify Your "Why"

What do you uniquely contribute to the Kingdom?

Who are you most burdened to serve or influence?

Purpose Statement Format:

"_____ [action verb or calling] _____ [eternal outcome or growth] _____ [people]."

Example: *Equip transformational leaders.*

Purpose Statement (1–2 sentences):

_____

_____

3. Define Your Mission

Your mission is your purpose in motion. It answers the *who* and *how* of your calling.

Why Your Mission is Significant:

It translates vision into action.

It guides your stewardship.

It simplifies decision-making.

It fuels momentum.

Process:

1. Define the people or groups you are called to serve.
2. Identify the main way you will serve them. Keep it clear and simple.

Example: "To equip others to walk in truth and live on mission."

Practical Step: Share your mission with a trusted friend or mentor for feedback and prayer.

Mission Statement (clear and simple):

_____

_____

4. Capture Your Vision

Vision paints a picture of what your life could look like if you fully trusted God and walked faithfully in your mission.

Why Vision is Critical:

Direction and endurance: Without vision, you drift or settle for survival mode.

Legacy shaping: The decisions you make today form the future you'll leave behind.

Multiplication: Vision isn't only about what you do—it's also about who you raise up.

Process:

Ask: *If I trusted God fully, what kind of difference could my life make over the next 10 years?*

Make it big enough to require God's power, not just your own effort.

Practical Step: Write a paragraph describing your future in vivid, faith-filled terms. Use present tense as if it is already happening.

Vision Paragraph (write as if it's already happening):

_____

_____

5. Name the Problem You Desire to Solve

Eternal impact happens when we bring the hope and truth of Christ into real human struggles. The Lord gives us different passions that can be used to help others in their challenges.

Process:
Identify who you are called to help.
Describe the primary struggle they face that you can help them overcome for God's glory.

Practical Step: Write one sentence:
"I help [specific people] overcome [specific struggle] so they can [eternal or redemptive outcome]."

Example: "I help young leaders overcome fear and confusion so they can live with courage and clarity in Christ."

Your Sentence:
"I help _____ overcome _____

so they can _____."

Chapter Eleven

Finishing Well to Entering into the Joy of the Master

"The joy of the Lord is the believer's inheritance, not merely for the future, but in full measure when we see Him face to face."
— Charles Spurgeon

"You make known to me the path of life; in your presence there is fullness of joy; at your right hand are pleasures forevermore."
— Psalm 16:11

Reflection: C.S. Lewis and The Weight of Glory

"To please God... to be a real ingredient in the divine happiness... to be loved by God, not merely pitied, but delighted in... seems impossible, a weight of glory which our thoughts can hardly sustain." — C.S. Lewis

"For this light momentary affliction is preparing for us an eternal weight of glory beyond all comparison." — 2 Corinthians 4:17

Lewis captures what words can barely contain: the staggering reality that our greatest joy is to be welcomed into God's presence and to hear His "Well done." This is not about vanity or self-congratulation—it is about the joy of being fully known, fully loved, and fully delighted in by our Creator.

Our longing for Heaven is not accidental. It is woven into our design so that we might seek the fullness of joy found only in God's presence (Psalm 16:11). The true reward of a faithful life is not recognition or legacy, but God's delight in our obedience (Matthew 25:21).

This truth reorders our priorities. It pulls us away from living for what fades tomorrow and fixes us on what lasts forever. It elevates the value of people—immortal souls who will outlast this world (1 Thessalonians 2:19-20). Even trials are not wasted; they prepare us for glory (Romans 8:18).

To live in light of this weight of glory means we:
>   Shift our motivation from pleasing people to pleasing God.
>   Make decisions and set priorities with eternity in view.
>   Value people deeply—encouraging, discipling, serving them with the end in mind.
>   Embrace trials as God's refining work shaping us for the joy to come.

"To please God... to be a real ingredient in the divine happiness... to be loved by God, not merely pitied, but delighted in... seems impossible, a weight of glory which our thoughts can hardly sustain." — C.S. Lewis

"For this light momentary affliction is preparing for us an eternal weight of glory beyond all comparison." — 2 Corinthians 4:17

Prayer: Lord, keep my eyes on the joy set before me—the joy of being with You, fully known and fully loved. Shape my life so that my greatest desire is to please You and to share in Your glory. Amen.

Making an Eternal Difference in Difficult Times – Well Done, Good and Faithful Servant

In a parable about the end times, Jesus offers a picture of what our lives should look like in face of challenges. He was facing His death, and He know the disciples had rough days ahead. Every believe has been given capabilities, opportunities and privileges. The Lord has invested in us. What do we do with what we have been given. The parable speaks to each giving an accounting. This reckoning & reward will be the focus of our next 4 sessions.

Matthew 25:21, 23, "'Well done, good and faithful slave. You were faithful with a few things; I will put you in charge of many things; enter into the joy of your master.'

Well Done

Well done" literally means *"Great job, now come be my partner."* It speaks to a life lived with excellence, integrity, and wholehearted devotion to God. To hear it is the deepest longing of the believer's heart.

But this commendation is not earned through sheer effort. The only path to "well done" is a vibrant relationship with Christ—a life of abiding, not striving (John 15:5). It is revealed through paradoxes: strength through weakness, life through death, greatness through servanthood.

To live a "well done" life is to:
Glorify the Lord – making Him known through worship, thanksgiving, and obedience.
Please the Lord – walking by faith (Hebrews 11:6), believing and acting in trust.
Work with excellence – doing our best as a reflection of God's character.
Be set apart – living distinctively, offering hope that causes the world to notice.
Finish well – persevering with purity and faithfulness to the end.

Good

"Good" in the parable means *useful, worthwhile, of high quality.* God evaluates not just what we do, but why we do it. Motive matters as much as outcome. We are called

We are to be and do all things with a Godly character. We are to do good, to help, and serve others. Be and do right, with quality, excellent, and skillful. *1 Thessalonians 4:1, "Finally then, brethren, we request and exhort you in the Lord Jesus, that as you received from us instruction as to how you ought to walk and please God (just as you actually do walk), that you excel still more.* Practically: Do the next, best, right thing

1 Corinthians 3:13-15 reminds us that each person's work will be tested by fire—what remains is reward, what burns up is loss. True goodness flows from a transformed heart, producing acts that are wholesome, reliable, helpful, and obedient.

The call is simple: ***"Do the next best right thing."***

Faithful

The word translated as "faithful" means "trustful", "obedient," "loyal," and "deserving belief, consistent, character, " It has both the sense of trusting someone else and being trustworthy. So, as we journey in the midst of morass, we are to be trustworthy, counted on, and consistent. Faithful implies both a relationship to the one you report to and to a world who is watching. We are to be faithful to the Lord and a world looking in.

Faithful and Faithfulness are central to the Christian life. It is a chief component for our eternal life. Source and example of faithfulness is the Lord. 1 Corinthians 1:9 *"God is faithful, by whom ye were called unto the fellowship of his"*

Faithfulness will determine what the Lord will give us in this life. Nothing is too small for the Lord to see. This includes actions as well as motives. The Lord is always watching, and He will reward us. That reward is the true riches (not money and possessions) such as experiencing love with the Lord, relationships, people, and blessings in this life.

Faithfulness will determine our eternal rewards in heaven which includes love, responsibility and crowns. Our life on earth will impact our eternity. Just because we can't see heaven does not mean that it does not exist and thus carries a consequence of behavior now. Matthew 6:19-21. Where our treasure is our heart will be also. Mother Teresa said, *'I do not pray for success. I ask for faithfulness.'*

Servant

Being a servant requires a mature depth of character in particular humility and security. Know that you are a "prisoner / slave" of Christ – first and foremost. Must be modeled as a living example. (141 times in the bible.) *"Give of your hands to serve and your hearts to love."* Mother Teresa

Jesus taught extensively about being a servant and serving others. Often the disciples wanting to know who was the greatest. You serve one master; you can't serve God and money. Need a pure and undivided heart.

Matthew 6:24, *""No one can serve two masters. Either you will hate the one and love the other, or you will be devoted to the one and despise the other. You cannot serve both God and money."*

Mark 9:34-35, *"for on the way they had discussed with one another which of them was the greatest.35 Sitting down, He called the twelve and *said to them, "If anyone wants to be first, he shall be last of all and servant of all."*

Implications
1. **Serving is central to discipleship.** In a self-promoting world, we embody Christ when we value others above ourselves.
2. **Calling and purpose fuel servanthood.** A clear sense of mission keeps us focused and resilient.
3. **Servanthood requires depth.** It demands humility, courage, faith, and love rooted in Christ.

Entering the Joy of Your Master — Living Eternity Now

These five shifts form the foundation of the transformed life. But the story doesn't end there. There is a final movement—a forward-looking, upward-calling, joy-filled reality that gives meaning to every moment: *"entering into the joy of your Master"* (Matthew 25:21). This is not just about finishing the race well; it's about finishing into someone—into Jesus. It's about living now, not as a far-off destination, but as a present and growing reality.

What Does It Mean to "Enter into the Joy of the Master"?

In Jesus' parable of the talents (Matthew 25:14–30), the master returns and says to the faithful servant, *"Well done, good and faithful servant... Enter into the joy of your master."* This phrase is often used at funerals, evoking the hope of heaven. But Jesus was offering more than just a future promise—He was describing the reward of a life that lives for and with the Master now. This joy is not simply a feeling—it is a condition of *union,* the result of a faithful relationship with Christ that flows from trust and love.

To enter into the joy of the Lord is to share in His delight, His purpose, and His presence. It is the full-hearted experience of being aligned with the will of God, being confident in His love, and being satisfied in His fellowship. It's the opposite of burnout, striving, performance, or religious exhaustion. It's not about what we've done *for* God—it's about what we've become *in* God. And it begins now, not just in heaven.

How Do We Live This Out Now?

The joy of the Master is not reserved for the moment we die—it is available to those who live in abiding union with Christ. In John 15:11, Jesus says, *"These things I have spoken to you, that My joy may be in you, and that your joy may be full."* What things had He spoken? The words about abiding in Him, letting His life flow through us, and bearing fruit as branches of the True Vine.

Here's how we begin to live it out now:
1. **Maintain constant fellowship.** Abiding, not occasional connection, fuels lasting joy.
2. **Rest in your identity as beloved.** Jesus was declared "beloved" before His ministry began; so are we.
3. **Obey as joy, not duty.** Obedience is not burdensome—it is the pathway to joy.
4. **Let eternity shape today.** Lewis reminds us: "Aim at heaven and you will get earth thrown in."

The Christian life is not about doing more *for* Jesus—it is about living more *with* Jesus. Not performance, but presence. Not legacy, but intimacy.

Why Is This So Meaningful?

Because it reframes what the Christian life is really about. The transformed life is not a call to do more for Jesus—it's a call to be more with Jesus. It's not about building a legacy; it's about preparing for an eternal relationship. When we shift from achievement to abiding, from performance to presence, we stop needing to be impressive and start becoming deeply formed.

This is the life of rest, trust, freedom, and eternal joy. We no longer measure ourselves by worldly standards, or by the approval of others. We live with the smile of God over our lives, content in His pleasure, joyful in His presence, and free to love without fear. In that space, we are fully alive.

But these shifts do not merely prepare us to live better lives. They prepare us to live eternal lives—the kind of life Jesus promised not just after death, but now, in Him. After these shifts, the Christian life is no longer focused on finishing well alone, but on something even more profound: *"entering into the joy of your Master"* (Matthew 25:21). This joy is the reward of intimacy with Christ—a joy that is both present and eternal, rooted not in outcomes but in union.

As we seek to finish well we live with perseverance which helps us work on the right priorities. Right living helps us avoid burnout. We reflect faithfulness in the process.

From Admiration to Abandonment: Dallas Willard's Surrender

Dallas Willard was admired as a brilliant philosopher, professor, and spiritual thinker. He spent decades teaching at the University of Southern California, deeply respected in both academic and church communities. But behind the public acclaim was a man who, like many others, had to undergo a quiet change—letting go not of intellect, but of *control*. A shift from striving to abide. From being admired to being abandoned to Christ.

Early in life, Willard had been a devout Christian, shaped by Baptist roots and a deep hunger for spiritual truth. But he eventually came to realize that much of what he had learned was shaped more by performance and moralism than by true inner transformation. Despite his intellect and reputation, he recognized that he had been living in what he called the "gospel of sin management"—trying to be better without becoming new.

In his writings and personal reflections, he described the turning point not as dramatic, but as deep. It was the moment when he realized that the Christian life was not about working harder to become like Jesus—but about surrendering fully so that Jesus could live through him.

"The revolution of Jesus is in the first place and continuously a revolution of the human heart." Dallas Willard, The Divine Conspiracy

That heart revolution happened in him. He surrendered the role of master and instead became a student—not just of Jesus' teachings, but of Jesus Himself.

Living Eternal Life Now

Dallas Willard's transformation reshaped his understanding of *eternal life*. He taught that eternal life is not just about where you go when you die, but about the kind of life you live now—a life lived in interactive relationship with the Father, Son, and Holy Spirit. In *The Divine Conspiracy*, he wrote: "Eternal life is not something that begins when we die. Eternal life is the life we are given from God that begins when we trust Him and live in His presence now."

This is the joy of the Master. It is not merely a heavenly reward—it is a present reality that comes from walking in a deep, sustained love with Jesus. It is the evidence of the four shifts. It is the culmination of coming to our end.

Willard would say that the transformed life is one in which every ordinary moment—writing, walking, cleaning, speaking—is done *with* Jesus, not just *for* Him. He believed that the greatest tragedy was not moral failure, but *spiritual drift*—a life lived out of alignment with the joy of the Kingdom. Dallas modeled a life that was both deeply contemplative and joyfully engaged. For him, the Christian life was not pressure, but participation in the very life of God.

Chapter Twelve

A Call to Action

"Only one life, 'twill soon be past, only what's done for Christ will last." — **Charles Spurgeon**

"But our citizenship is in heaven. And we eagerly await a Savior from there, the Lord Jesus Christ." — **Philippians 3:20**

"The world and its desires pass away, but whoever does the will of God lives forever." — **1 John 2:17**

A Call to Action

This is your invitation: Lay down the life we're trying to control—and receive the life Christ died to give us. Trying harder hasn't worked. What if surrendering deeper is the only way forward? We were never meant to carry the weight of our spiritual life. We weren't redeemed to feel this stuck. If nothing changes… nothing changes. Trying harder doesn't work, it never has. Live is about trusting. Jesus didn't just come to save us—He came to live His life in us. We need a new operating system powered by Jesus Christ. These five shifts in thinking are a way to foster deeper growth in your ongoing walk with the Lord that will bring a fresh sense of His presence.

The Consequence

If we don't make these shifts, life will continue to be a grind. We'll keep trying to do right, serving, striving—and wondering why joy feels distant becoming spiritually dry, and rest is out of reach. Without these shifts, we'll stay busy on the outside but feel bankrupt on the inside - stuck in shame, guilt, and exhaustion. The result? We will continue in bondage having been conformed to the patterns of this world. It is struggle or death - there is no middle ground. The longer we delay these shifts the deeper hole we will dig.

Made for More

When we embrace these shifts, we'll walk in the freedom Christ promised. Not just someday in heaven—but here and now. We will stop striving and start abiding:

From **surviving** to **breakthrough**
From **religion** to **relationship**
From **trying harder** to **trusting deeper**
From **busyness** to a **multiplying impact**

This is the Christian life, not you living for Christ, but Christ alive in us. Not a better version of us, it is a new creation in Him. This is not about fixing our life but receiving His.

Responding to God's Initiative

The Lord is always at work in the world and is calling us into His eternal purposes and plans. There are four ways the Lord is working to engage us:

A Call from Above - The Lord wants us to engage by responding to His calls us to Himself and then to His Great Commission.

A Cry from Around – The pain and hurts of people around show us a world in need of Christ.

An Agony from Below – The eternal separation from God by people who never followed should give us an urgency to share.

An Urge to Go Out – We all are called to be beacons of light with a message of hope to those in need.

We do these by getting beyond ourselves and trying to meet our needs and desires, but shift our focus to helping others who need Christ and need to grow in Christ and in doing so moves us to an eternal perspective and action.

Practical Action

To realize this living for what is eternal will take priorities of focus and discipline of activity. The simple view of what is most important is making time for and pursuing a love relationship with the Lord. Secondly, it is to grow in having a biblical view of life to make wise and strategic decisions. Thirdly, is to invest your life in people – sharing Christ, discipling and mentoring fellow followers and adding value to all who you serve. Live your life fully with no regrets and you will be amazed at the blessings you will have.

Summary

1. **Heart – Who? (Faith / Love)**

    The journey begins with the heart, where we realize who we truly are. The shift is from a **Christ-like life**—mere imitation of His example—to the **Christ-life**, His indwelling presence expressed through us. The call is to die to self and surrender daily, allowing His love to flow unhindered. When we appropriate Christ's life in place of our own striving, we experience the eternal reality of His unfailing love. *"I have been crucified with Christ. It is no longer I who live, but Christ lives in me"* (Gal. 2:20). Let your heart not merely try harder, but yield deeper—where imitation ends, transformation begins.

    "The Christian life is not difficult; it is impossible. It must be the life of Christ in us." — Major Ian Thomas

2. Purpose – Why? (Hope)

Purpose answers the question of why we exist: to know Him and make Him known. The great shift is from doing things **for Christ to living *from* Christ**—drawing on His life as the source of our strength and meaning. This means abiding in Him, not in our own efforts, and bearing fruit that remains. When we live from this rooted place, the eternal Word shapes our lives and impacts others long after we are gone. Let your life be anchored in abiding hope and the Living Word, not restless striving.

"The will of God will never take you where the grace of God cannot keep you." — Hudson Taylor

3. Gifts – What? (Blessings)

Every gift in life is a blessing entrusted, not earned. The shift is from **achieving** through self-effort to **receiving** with gratitude. Out of that posture, we give freely to others as stewards, not owners. Thanksgiving opens the hand of blessing, and generosity releases eternal promise. What we receive from God is never meant to terminate on ourselves, but to be sown for eternal fruit. Don't hoard your blessings; let them flow through you into the lives of others.

"You have not lived today until you have done something for someone who can never repay you." — John Bunyan

4. Work – How? (Light)

Work is the arena where faith meets action. The shift is from **king**—building our own small empires—to **kingdom**—serving Christ's greater reign with excellence. Whatever our craft, vocation, or calling, we serve not as unto men but as unto the Lord. True excellence is not perfectionism but faithfulness; it is the light of Christ revealed in everyday labor. When we work with kingdom vision, people are eternally impacted. Your work is worship; do it well, do it unto Him.

"Work as if everything depended upon you, but pray as if everything depended upon God." — Ignatius of Loyola

5. **Suffering – When? (Persevere)**

Suffering asks when we will trust God—only in blessing, or also in pain? The shift is from seeing trials as obstacles to embracing them as pathways to triumph. God uses hardship to mature us, refine our faith, and display His glory through us. Perseverance in suffering is not resignation but transformation, and the eternal outcome is a share in Christ's glory. Do not waste your suffering—let it be the furnace in which your faith shines.

"If you are suffering, rejoice because you are being made like Christ. The cross is never greater than the grace." — Charles Spurgeon

So here is the call: **Live for what lasts.**
 Surrender your heart, Posses Christ.
 Abide in Him and His purposes.
 Be thankful and give your gifts away
 Serve with your work faithfully
 Persevere through suffering with Joy

Each shift moves you from the temporal to the eternal, from striving to surrender, from your story to His.

The temporary will fade, but Christ, His Word, His promises, His people, and His glory will remain forever. The invitation is clear: live now in light of then. To do so, we must count the cost. **Eternity is at stake.**

Counting the Cost

A key part of "living for what lasts" involves counting the cost. Jesus explains this in Luke 14:26-35.

"If anyone comes to Me, and does not hate his own father and mother and wife and children and brothers and sisters, yes, and even his own life, he cannot be My disciple. ²⁷Whoever does not carry his own cross and come after Me cannot be My disciple. ²⁸For which one of you, when he wants to build a tower, does not first sit down and calculate the cost to see if he has enough to complete it?

²⁹Otherwise, when he has laid a foundation and is not able to finish, all who observe it begin to ridicule him, ³⁰saying, 'This man began to build and was not able to finish.' ³¹Or what king, when he sets out to meet another king in battle, will not first sit down and consider whether he is strong enough with ten thousand men to encounter the one coming against him with twenty thousand? ³²Or else, while the other is still far away, he sends a delegation and asks for terms of peace.

³³So then, none of you can be My disciple who does not give up all his own possessions.

³⁴"Therefore, salt is good; but if even salt has become tasteless, with what will it be seasoned? ³⁵It is useless either for the soil or for the manure pile; it is thrown out. He who has ears to hear, let him hear."

He was challenging the disciples to the cost of discipleship which is not an easy route and most definitely be a painful route. Paul outlines four areas of the counting of the cost: 1. the priorities of relationships - choosing between Christ and family members, 2. You must count the cost of carrying your own cross – dying to self, 3. the cost when building - you count the cost before you build and thus not have enough to finish and 4. if you do not of up all your own possessions you'll not be a disciple of mine

Jesus challenged the followers to be fully commited and it will be costly, painful and yet. there will be reward in heaven. And if we invest in things in the world with the right motive that honors the Lord and do things with a faithful stewardship attitude that will accrue an eternal result. But if we spend our money and resources on pleasure or status or any other means it does not lift up Christ it will accrue no value in eternity. So the call is clear, invest in God's purposes with God's motive and it will produce things of eternal value.

Counting the Cost

1. Love Christ so much that any other love appears as hate. → RELATIONSHIPS
2. Carry his own Cross and. come after Christ → PURPOSE
3. Building and Finishing → WORK
4. Give up all his own possessions → POSSESSIONS

Have you counted the cost? What price are willing you to pay?

Final Truth

We weren't made to perform our way to peace. We were made to walk in union with the living Christ. This isn't self-help in Christian wrapping. This is the restoration of design—God's design for how life was always meant to work: through Him. We don't need to become more like Christ. We need Christ to become more visible through us.

We were made for more – much more. The Lord has designed us to experience an ever-deepening intimacy with Him that is the well spring of joy, peace, and fulfillment, He has created us for meaningful relationships with others so that we don't go through alone in our struggle or pain. Finally, He has provided each of us with gifts so we can participate in His purposes with supernatural power.

A Final Call to Live for What Lasts

The life you've been given is brief, but its impact can reverberate into eternity. Heaven's perspective changes everything—it redefines what is significant, how you spend your time, where you place your hope, and what you treasure most. This is the essence of living for what lasts—keeping your eyes on the eternal, even while your feet are firmly planted in today's responsibilities.

Charles Spurgeon cuts to the heart of it: *"If Christ be anything, He must be everything."* Colossians 3:17 says it plainly: *"And whatever you do, whether in word or deed, do it all in the name of the Lord Jesus..."* The call is total—every thought, every decision, every action centered on Him. So, as you close these pages, choose today to live for what lasts. Give God the first and best of your time, treasure, and talents. Love people deeply because their souls will last forever. Let your daily choices reflect eternal priorities.

The Christ life is already inside us. Now it's time to live like it. The clock is ticking, the opportunities are precious, and eternity is real. Live now so that when you see your Lord face to face, you will hear the words that will make every sacrifice worth it. *"Well done, good and faithful servant... Enter into the joy of your master."*

ABOUT THE AUTHOR

Bruce R. Witt is President of Leadership Revolution Inc., a non-profit organization dedicated to developing and multiplying servant leaders to reach their world. He began his career in marketing for Shell Oil Company in the solid plastics area. He was led to join the Christian Business Men's Committee where he directed the U.S. field operations and authored several key curriculum for the ministry, including the Operation Timothy spiritual development series and the Lighthouse evangelism curriculum.

In 2008, after seeing the tremendous need for leaders to understand and practice successful leadership principles, Bruce was led to form Leadership Revolution in order to establish a process that would help leaders.

Bruce has written curriculum and training resources and he regularly travels throughout the United States and the globe conducting workshops, conferences and train the trainer sessions to spread the vision and empower others. Along with partner organizations and churches, Bruce has trained thousands of leaders and trained hundreds of trainers who can also train others.

Bruce has been married to his wife Dana for 40 years and they have two grown sons—Robert, married to Allison, and Andrew, married to Amy, who have three sons: Brooks, Harrison, and Cooper.

NOTES

NOTES

NOTES

NOTES

NOTES

ABOUT LEADERSHIP REVOLUTION INC.

THE PROBLEM is there's a leadership crisis, and current leadership training isn't working.

THE SOLUTION is that we begin with Christ as the One Leader. His infinite, supernatural power is released through brokenness and surrender.

OUR MISSION is to establish Christ as the One Leader in every follower. Our Vision is to transform leaders in every contisent to multiply the Gospel impact.

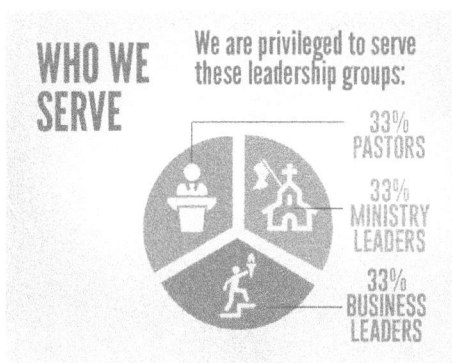

We train leaders along with 16 strategic partners to follow the One Leader, Jesus Christ, and His model of leadership. We're blessed to serve and train in 17 countries including Egypt, India, Ghana, Kenya, Indonesia, Russia, China, and several Latin American countries.

Whether it's training your staff on the One Leader message or joining us as a partner in Ministry, please contact us to learn more.

LeadershipRevolution.us | 678-637-9890 | Bruce@LeadershipRevolution.us

Leadership Revolution Inc. is a 501(c)3 nonprofit.
All gifts and donations are tax deductible.

MORE RESOURCES FROM LEADERSHIP REVOLUTION

Many give a mental assent to this teaching yet are often asking, "What do I do? What does Christ as life look like?" Too often Christians err by moving too far to one side or the other—reducing the Christian life to a list of do's and don'ts, or they actually do nothing. These inspiring weekly devotions are just some of the actions that reflect the life of Christ in each of us.

ISBN 978-1-7328200-0-5
144 pages, Softcover

Everyone faces mountains and valleys in life—that is a fact. The question is how do we experience victory in them? We can have triumph in Christ in every circumstance! Is this too good to be true? Is it some overly positive mental attitude, or can it be a reality? This is a book about living with hope in life's difficulties and progressing while doing well.

ISBN 978-0-9965714-9-4
168 pages, Softcover

Order from Amazon.com or www.LeadershipRevolution.us

www.ingramcontent.com/pod-product-compliance
Lightning Source LLC
Chambersburg PA
CBHW070501100426
42743CB00010B/1708